MORNING SERMONS

MORNING SERMONS

BY

GEORGE H. MORRISON, D.D.

BAKER BOOK HOUSE
Grand Rapids, Michigan

Reprinted 1971 by
Baker Book House Company

ISBN: 0-8010-5890-2

PREFACE

In the foreword to his first published volume of addresses (*Flood-Tide*) my husband explained that these were written ' after the more severe preparations for the forenoon diet of worship were got through.'

No collection of his morning sermons has ever appeared, and these, which were all preached in Wellington Church, Glasgow, are offered in response to requests from many quarters.

I am deeply grateful to Dr. Hubert L. Simpson of Westminster Church, London, for his help in bringing out this book ; also for his friendship and ministry, and because in Westminster I have found during the last two years so much to strengthen, so much to remind me of Wellington.

CHRISTINE MORRISON.

INTRODUCTION

"Dr. George Herbert Morrison has a gift of saying things that we all would have said, had it occurred to us to say them; and he said those inevitable things as we could not, in English prose that had the effect of poetry on the heart." This quotation of James Denney aptly sums up the "secret" — if there was such a thing — of Dr. Morrison's classic sermons delivered from his pulpit in Wellington Church, Glasgow, Scotland, from 1902 to 1928.

Throughout his ministry he was known for his concentrated study, his regular pastoral visitation, and his constant writing for publication. His appeal lay not in any physical stature, for he lacked that; not in any tricks or oratory, for he never preached for effect; but in the quiet winsome way in which he spoke to the heart from a heart suffused with the love and grace of Christ. He never lost sight of the fact that as a minister of Christ his first concern must be how best to bring his hearers closer to the heart of the Lord.

Although some fifty years old now, his sermons are modern in touch and spirit; the tone and temper are admirably effective for use today. Their simplicity of phrase came out of arduous toil as the writer worked in his preparation. The style is the man — quiet and genial — and his preaching was like this. Morrison was always the pastor-preacher, ever seeking to meet life's needs with some word from God.

Whatever he did had the hallmark of preparation and finality. Some sermons came easily like the bird on the wing; others came after much hard work and sweat of mind and heart. The fact that he brooded over his texts with something of an artist's unconsciousness and superb leisure is one of the elements in his power as a preacher. He brooded over the Word of God until it became translucent. His loyalty to Christ and his devotion in the secret place are wedded to his daily practice of study and writing.

His counsel to the young preacher is most revealing as the secret of his own success: "I can think of nothing, except that young preachers will do well to guard against the tendency to rush which is the bane of modern life. The habit of unprofitable bustle and rush, the present-day preoccupation with small affairs and engagements, is withholding many good things from us. For myself it is essential that I have leisure to brood and meditate."

To read and study these selections from the author's many volumes of messages will be to open new vistas of truth and to learn how old and familiar truths can be clothed in fresh and living words which will glow with unsuspected meaning.

Ralph G. Turnbull

GEORGE H. MORRISON, D.D.

It used to be said that just as visitors to London in bygone days felt that they must of necessity hear Spurgeon or Parker or Liddon, so visitors to Glasgow in more recent years had the feeling that they could not miss hearing Dr. George H. Morrison in Wellington Church. One of the most noted of English Bishops, after fulfilling an afternoon engagement at the University, hurried off to be in time for the evening service at Wellington. And the miner from Fifeshire, or the crofter from the Hebrides, spending a Sunday in Glasgow, would have considered the day incomplete if he did not hear Dr. Morrison.

To Glasgow Dr. Morrison's ministry at Wellington

was something like what Dr. Alexander Whyte's ministry at St. George's was to Edinburgh. Different in many ways, they were alike in the extent to which they captured the community and maintained their unbroken hold year after year.

Dr. Morrison was a great preacher who was also a great pastor. Of this rather unusual combination he was, indeed, the supreme example.

His genius as a preacher was never more clearly shown than by his success in solving the problem of the second service. Shortly after his settlement in Glasgow, the afternoon service was giving place to an evening one, but the results in general were not too satisfactory. When Wellington decided on an evening service Dr. Morrison was determined to give it a distinctive character. In the mornings he adhered to the old Scottish tradition of expository preaching.

In the evenings he allowed himself a wider scope, presenting the Christian essentials in a somewhat different setting, and, as he said, calling to his help every type of illustrative aid that appealed to him. He strove to give these evening addresses a strong human interest, in order, as he put it, "to win the attention, in honourable ways, of some at least of the vast class of people who sit very loosely to the Church. The touch is naturally far lighter than in the morning, but this does not mean lack of preparation. I prepare as carefully for the one as for the other." His one aim in preaching, he once said, was "to help people along the road." Here I may interpolate how Dr. Morrison once told me that, after he had fully prepared his subject, he set himself the task of striving to see how simply he could present it. His simplicity, therefore, was not the easy, facile thing some may have supposed it to be; it was the fruit of definite and earnest effort.

The response at his evening service was immediate and striking. The church became crowded to overflowing, long queues formed in University Avenue before the doors were opened and this was no mere passing phase. The same state of matters continued for over twenty-six years, right to the end of his ministry. And he got the class of people he set out to reach. These crowded evening congregations at Wellington made an interesting study in themselves. All classes and all ages were represented, but young men and women were always largely in evidence. Nor were they there because of the prospect of any novelty or sensation. They could only have been drawn because they felt that their wistful longings and inarticulate yearnings were somehow met and answered by the man in the pulpit with the soft voice, the quiet effortless style, and the subtle elusive charm.

There was no clangorous or challenging presentation of a new Evangel. Dr. Morrison's secret was in taking old familiar truths and clothing them in fresh robes of language which made them sparkle with a lustre of their own and revealed meanings hitherto hidden and unsuspected. He had a perfect flair in the selection of texts often fresh and suggestive. "He gave them drink out of the depths," "In the day that thou stoodest on the other side," "The deep that croucheth beneath," "Thou didst cleave the earth with rivers," are some that may be quoted, almost at random.

Many of his sermons were prose poems; all of them were suffused with a tender charm and rich in spiritual helpfulness. Volume after volume was published, and G. H. Morrison's sermons found a place in manse libraries everywhere, almost like those of F. W. Robertson, of Brighton, while they also very markedly appealed to a wide circle of lay readers. They revealed him to be both a mystic and a man of letters, and were acknowledged to place him in the foremost ranks of British preachers. . . .

There are many people who still remember this or that sermon of Dr. Morrison's; there are as many who love to recall instances of his pastoral devotion. His routine visitation, so extensive and incessant, was but one feature of his pastoral activity. Many tales could be told of his constant solicitous care of the sick and those in sorrow or trouble. And no success or joy that came to any member of any family in his congregation was overlooked or allowed to pass without letters or postcards from him, which are still prized possessions.

The end of this notable ministry came swiftly and unexpectedly when Dr. Morrison was at the age of sixty-two, and while there was no sign of any waning of his powers and no abatement of his popularity. In the first week of October, 1928, he was back from his summer holiday — he held that a good holiday was a *sine qua non* for a minister — and he was getting into the full stream of another winter's activities. On the Wednesday afternoon he had spent three continuous hours in the homes of his people, and in the evening he gave a memorable address to a small company of workers in the hall of Gorbals Church. On Thursday evening he became seriously ill, and on Sunday morning shortly after midnight he passed away, almost before his illness had become generally known.

On the day before he died, when there was a slight rally, he was able to have in his hands one of the early copies of a book to which he had been looking forward — his biography, which I had written at the request of London publishers, and in the preparation of which he had given me every facility with his characteristic kindness.

Although Dr. Morrison did not reach the allotted span, he, if any man, had done what he used to call "a good day's darg." He warned young preachers against unprofitable bustle and rush, and preoccupation with small affairs and trifling engagements. A master of method, he so ordered his time that, while he was never idle, he was never hurried or flurried. There was always about him a calm serenity, and as he moved among men he seemed a living epistle of what he preached.

Reprinted from Alexander Gammie, *Preachers I Have Heard*, Pickering & Inglis, Ltd. (London, n.d.)

CONTENTS

PAGE

AT a period not far distant from the present, and well within the memory of some of us, it was the fashion to decry all truth that was not reached by the action of the intellect. The only interpretation reckoned valid was an intellectual interpretation. The only methods which were regarded seriously were the logical and scientific. The only truths deemed worthy of acceptance were such as were capable of comprehension and could be verified by scientific processes.

For this insistence on the comprehensible, there were reasons which are readily apparent. There was that wonderful awakening of the intellect that marked the nineteenth century in England ; there were those marvellous discoveries of science which gave to science a certain lordly arrogance as if there were no truths she could not come by, and no secrets she could not penetrate. All that was only a little while ago, and yet one is conscious of a subtle change to-day. The sense of mystery which broods on things is far more vivid than thirty years ago. Men are awakening as to haunting presences which are ever near us yet eluding us ; they feel that there are more things in heaven and earth than are dreamed of in our philosophy. There is a growing belief that in the universe are secrets which are not intellectual at all. There is a strengthening trust in the verdict of the feelings and in the illumination of the will. There is a deepening sense that all that is most real can never be demonstrated by any logic, but must be felt where argument is hushed in the silence and the shadow of the soul.

Now this new attitude of men and women is what may be called the attitude of mysticism. He who feels so, although he may not know it, has been touched by the flaming of the mystic torch. And it is on that mysticism, and the gains of it in the peculiar circumstances of the hour, that I wish to speak a word or two this morning.

Taken in its most general sense, mysticism may be defined in some such way as this. It is the attitude of mind that feels intensely the wonder and the mystery of things. There is a little poem by Tennyson which I may read to you, as beautifully illustrative of this attitude :—

' Flower in the crannied wall,
  I pluck you out of the crannies ;—
  I hold you here, root and all, in my hand,
  Little flower—but if I could understand
  What you are, root and all, and all in all,
  I should know what God and man is.'

Well now, in regard to nature, that is the typical mystic attitude. The mystic's finger is on the skirts of God when he touches the flower in the crannied wall. The botanist classifies it in the realm of nature ; the artist revels in its perfect colouring ; the mystic finds in it, beneath its beauty, the shadow of the unseen and the eternal. For him there is a spirit eager to express itself in every bird that flies and every flower that opens ; for him there is more in the cataract than water, and more in the sunshine than a little kindly heat. For him all nature is a sacrament, the outward sign and seal of the invisible, the charactered garment of the eternal God, woven exquisitely upon the loom of time. The mystic has no quarrel with the man of science. He may himself be a scientific man, but he holds that reality has many aspects of which the scientific aspect is but one, and he claims for all those other aspects, which appeal to feelings rather than intelligence, a place in the interpretation of the whole. The mystic knows that all the sounds of music are but so many vibrations of the ether ; he knows that the whole range of melody can be thus scientifically accounted for ; but when he listens to the boyish chorister, whose voice goes ringing through the vast cathedral, when he hears the pealing of the solemn organ and the psalm that rises from a thousand hearts, when he hears the music of the forest or of the laverock lilting wildly down the glen, he knows there is more in music than vibrations. He does not doubt the scientific fact, but that fact is not the truth for him. For him the truth is all that flow of feeling that is liberated by the touch of melody. It is the wistful longing, the dim and vague regret, the visions of peace and purity and God that rise upon him out of the obscure night when the sound of music steals upon the ear. For the true mystic these are the realities, and all that he touches and sees is but a shadow. The everlasting hills are not so real to him as the mysterious peace of God which they convey. Some one is calling where the winds are sighing, some one is moving where the leaves are rustling, some one is yearning towards the human heart where the waves are breaking on the shore.

But mysticism is something more than that if we take it in its religious sense. It is the doctrine that God is to be sought and found in the

secret places of the soul. Not in the outward
world, however beautiful, is the true vision of
God to be attained. Sunrise and sunset and
the evening star—these are but the outskirts of
His ways. It is in the soul within us, in the
hidden sanctuary, in the silence and secret of
the human heart that the union which is true
blessedness is won, and the vision is granted
which is peace. For this end, says the mystic,
must a man learn to withdraw into himself.
He must learn to practise, whatever pain it cost
him, the spiritual method of detachment. He
must shut the gates on every chariot wheel and
close the lattice against the show of things, and
so, in silence and alone and self-absorbed, shall
he awaken to the fact of God. As on a summer
day on the hillside we watch the ships that are
sailing on the sea and mark the cottage smoke
that clambers heavenward, and follow the
wagons on the distant road, and so gradually
we fall a-dreaming and the active power of
vision is relaxed, and then, and not till then,
there steals upon us a murmuring as of a million
wings, so that we lose our hold on what is outward, seeing everything, as it were, yet seeing
nothing, so does there steal on the soul the mystic
sense of God. At first it may only be an intuition, a feeling inexplicable that He is here.
For most of us (poor worldlings that we are) it

may never be anything more wonderful than that, but for the heaven-born mystic that inward sense of God attains to such a glory of assurance, that like the apostle he is caught up into heaven and hears what human lips can never utter. Now it is just here that the difference comes in between all pagan and true Christian mysticism, and this is a matter of such profound importance that I would give much to make it clear to you. The great accusation levelled at the mystic is that he has no room for Jesus Christ. Alone with the infinite in secret rapture, the figure of the historic Jesus vanishes. But it has always seemed to me that this objection might equally be urged against the grace of prayer, for I question if anybody, when he prays to God, is actually conscious of the historic Christ. We do not go back in thought when we are praying to Him who walked among the fields of Galilee. We lift up our hearts without a thought of Galilee, to the Infinite and Eternal, and yet in so doing we glorify Jesus Christ, for all that we seek, and all that we find, in God, is what we have been taught to seek and find in the life and in the words of Christ. Now as it is with the exercise of prayer, so is it with the attitude of mysticism. A pagan mystic withdraws into the silence alone, unbefriended, unaccompanied, but a

Christian mystic withdraws into the silence with all that he has learned in Jesus Christ of a God who has a father's heart, and who knows the yearning of a father's love. Like the poor prodigal, the Christian mystic says, 'I will arise and go unto my father,' and so he arises from the world of sense, and goes to the quiet homeland of his soul. And there he is met in silence and in secret—not by a cold and unintelligible spirit, but by a Father who has never ceased to love, and loving, has never ceased to hope. There may be no consciousness of Jesus there, yet all the time Jesus is glorified. It is His God the Christian mystic meets and not any spirit of universal nature, and what I impress on you is this, that it is just at that point that the Christian mystic differs with a difference unspeakable from every Pantheist and Neoplatonist. That is the mysticism of St. Paul, and that is the mysticism of St. John. The pagan mystic whom they knew so well entered the secret place with empty hands, but they, out of the garden of the church, went in and locked the door and were alone, but they carried on their breast the Rose of Sharon and in the hand the Lily of the Valley.

One great service which mysticism renders is to keep religion from rigidity. When the Church is in danger of becoming hard, mysticism exerts a softening power. There are times when the Church is very dry and doctrinal, with clear-cut answers to every human problem, and men may seek refuge for the life of faith then in the beauty of ritual or the joy of praise, but the true salvation from a cold dogmatism is the breath of a mystical spirit in the Church, and the opening of eyes of awe upon the infinite, and the wondering spirit of a little child. When I was sent, a young minister, to Thurso, I found myself in a very strange environment. I found myself among a people to whom the doctrines of the faith were everything, and gradually, true Scotsman that I was, I found myself revelling in these dogmatic things, and able to split a hair with any of them on election and foreknowledge and freewill. But I had one friend there who was a perfect mystic as surely as he was a perfect gentleman. He is still there, rich in the inward light, though he has fallen on loneliness and blindness, and I bear my witness how that mystic saved me when my religion was becoming intellectual, and showed me how, with all our definitions, we must be still and know that He is God. In some such way, I think, in every age, has mysticism been a blessing to the Church. It has softened outlines, it has moved the heart, it has kept the truth from being stern and rigid. It has gone out from council and assembly where creeds were fashioned and heresies condemned, and it has remembered that even at the Cross there was darkness from the sixth hour to the ninth.

In mysticism, again, there is a refuge from our modern critical unsettlement. In a day of unsettlement and bewilderment like this, it is a refuge from the storm and a shadow from the heat. There was a time not so long ago when the record of Holy Scripture was unquestioned. Every page was verbally inspired and every statement had a divine authority. But now that old security has gone, and a thousand questions are asked about the Bible, and much that seemed fixed as the eternal hills is felt to be contingent and provisional. It was easy once to have a living faith based on the impregnable rock of Holy Scripture. It is easy still for all who play the traitor to the light which knowledge is pouring on the world. But it is not easy for the honest man who welcomes light whatever it discloses, and yet who feels that life is simply meaningless without the fellowship of Jesus Christ. How to be certain when all things seem uncertain, how to be fixed when everything seems shifting, that is the difficulty which thousands feel who are touched with the critical spirit of to-day, and it is just

there, it seems to me, that Christian mysticism
has its place and value, making it possible, amid
all unsettlement, to have a life of joy and power
and peace ; for mysticism does not go to Holy
Scripture with any theory of inspiration ; it
does not go to find any doctrines there or to
prove or disprove anything at all, but it goes to
the Bible with a childlike heart, bent upon finding some one who is calling, and having found
Him it opens wide the heart to Him and says,
' Come in, thou blessed of the Lord.' As when
a storm is raging on the sea, and in that storm
is some one whom we love, and we can hardly
see him for the driving mist, and yet we know
he is yonder on the waters, and so are we
fearful and smitten to the heart till he make the
shore and we clasp him in our arms, and then
we are no longer fearful but can look on the
crested waters and be still, so when once out
of the stormy sea we have drawn Christ into
the secret place, then for us there is no terror in
the tempest.   And remember that that is
always possible, no matter what our view of
Scripture is.   There is Christ arising from its
pages, mysterious, ineffable, sublime.   Take
Him in, my brother, to thine heart.   Don't ask
if the Bible be the Word of God : the Bible is the
Word of God to you if it brings you face to face
with Jesus Christ.

Lastly, and in a word or two, there is this further need to-day for Christian mysticism : it is God's corrective for that intense activity which is so characteristic of the modern Church. Whatever men may say about the Church, she is tremendously active and energetic. At home, abroad, in the slums of every city, she is toiling with an inspired assiduity, and ministers have such multifarious engagements that hardly can they snatch a quiet hour, and men and women have so many meetings that they have scarcely time to meet with God. Of all the blessings of this immense activity there is no one more thankfully cognisant than I am. It has called into action innumerable gifts and made many a wilderness blossom as the rose, and yet in the glow and fervour of that spirit there is one peril that is always imminent, and that is the peril lest the Church forget that she must be still and know that He is God. It is so much easier to bustle than to brood, it is so much easier to strive than to be still, it is so much easier to take the outward road than deliberately to take the inward road. And it is thus that a true Christian mysticism is needed to balance our clamorous activities, for in quietness and confidence shall be our strength. I look with all the desire of my heart for the spiritual revival that is coming. I am confident that I shall live to see the day when, like doves to their windows, men shall flock to Christ. But of this I am sure, that that day will not dawn till we have less faith in outward organisings, and a far deeper and more powerful faith in the broodings of the Holy Ghost. Whenever the Church relies on her committees, whenever she begins to be proud of her machinery, whenever she forgets in social zeal to wonder and be still and to adore, then mysticism comes, and like a breath from heaven falls on the cheek of all her fevered striving and bids her seek beatitude of rest. ' Be still and know that I am God,' she says. He leadeth the sheep by waters that are still. Not in the whirlwind is God manifested ; He speaks to the weaned heart in the still voice, and when He speaks, and when at last we hear Him, the thirsty land shall become springs of water, and the ransomed of the Lord shall come to Zion with songs and everlasting joy upon their heads.

II

'God delivered His strength into captivity.'—Ps. lxxviii. 61.

THESE words, in their primary and historical reference, refer to the passage which we read this morning, that is, the taking captive of the Ark of God by the Philistines. We saw in the chapter which we read what a terrific calamity that seemed to Israel. They thought that the glory of Israel had departed. You see, to the whole world it looked as if God were overcome; it looked as if some power had arisen that was really superior to God ; it looked as if there was something in the world that would ultimately baffle and defeat His purposes. You can understand how, to a religious nation like the Jews, even apart from the national calamity, that was a tremendous and terrifying thought, as of course it ought to be to every man. And then this inspired writer comes along, with his thought illuminated by the divine Spirit, and he puts a different complexion on the whole thing, tells you that God meant it, says to you in his own poetic language that God, nobody else, *God* delivered His strength into captivity. Don't you see in a moment how that thought would animate and inspire Israel? It was not that enemies had defeated God, it was that God had deliberately done it. God had not exercised His own omnipotence ; God had self-limited Himself. And that is one of the first glimpses of the great thought that is much occupying men's minds to-day. I suppose that every age has its own key with which it tries to unlock the problems and the difficulties of our universe, and I do not think it would be too much to say that the key which men are turning in the lock to-day is the key of the self-limiting of God. And I thought it my duty —as I like to make everything that men are thinking of familiar to my congregation—I thought it my duty, though the task is not easy, to try and show you what is meant to-day by that great thought which men are using so much—the thought of the self-limiting of God. It is so helpful, it is so explanatory of many of our problems and our mysteries, it is so fitted to safeguard the glory of God (and you and I are here just to glorify God), that if we could only understand how God, not only with the Ark, for that was typical, but right down the centuries, has delivered voluntarily His strength into captivity, I think it might confirm our faith.

Well now, suppose you take that thought

in regard to God's sovereign will. The one jubilant note of the whole Bible is that God's will in itself is sovereign. ' I formed the light and I created the darkness.' ' I am God and there is none beside Me.' Nobody who imagines that there is any will in the universe that can ever ultimately thwart God, nobody who imagines that, is making the Bible his rule of faith and life. Of course that does not mean that God's will is arbitrary. God cannot do many things just because He is love. As Butler said in his own deep way, ' God's being is a kind of law to His working.' All God's workings must be love if He is love. But it does mean that God's will in itself is irresistible, that nothing can ever ultimately baffle it, that there is no rival in heaven or in hell who can ever stand against the will of God. Don't you see how that thought is bound up with the ringing note of triumph of the Bible? You have got no assurance for the future unless you have got that ; not only for the future of the world, but for the future of yourself, and yourself strangely corresponds to the greater progress of the world. What a great comfort when a man can say, ' This is the will of God, even our sanctification.' Poor, weak sinners baffled every day, it is God's will that ultimately we will be clothed in white. But if God's will can be thwarted, if

there are powers abroad that make it not sovereign, why, you and I in every effort may be just
beating the air. Nothing may come of it. You
know that makes life impossible, and therefore
all the deeps in your heart corroborate the
jubilant assurance of the Bible, and if it did not
it would not be the Bible, because the deepest
mark of inspiration is within, and if the Bible
did not correspond with all the voices out of the
deeps of your heart, you might lay it aside, it
would not be inspired. But when you come to
the Lord Jesus, you find the Lord Jesus teaching
us to pray, ' Thy will be done.' Now if God's
will is an irresistible will, and if it is always
exercised as an irresistible will, why should you
and I pray, ' Thy will be done ' ? It will be
done whether you pray or not, it will be done
whether you help or not. It must be done if it
is exercised as a sovereign will. Don't you see
you are faced by this dilemma, though nobody
likes the argument of a dilemma, either the will
of God is not omnipotent (a thought that is
intolerable to the human heart) or else for wise,
holy purposes, when God is dealing with mankind, He does not exercise His sovereign will—
' He delivers His strength into captivity.' And
don't you see what His wise and holy purposes
are ? My father, when I was a boy, used to
spend his leisure in editing books, and I remem-

ber once, just when I was leaving school, he was editing one of the cantos of *Childe Harold*. He had the introduction all shaped out and most of his notes were blocked, and he turned to me and said : 'I am very busy, I want you to complete the editing of this book for me.' You know, to this hour, I have never forgotten it. To this hour I remember the joy and pride I felt when I was called to be a fellow-worker with my father. And if God's will for mankind were sovereign, if it just *had* to be, you could not be a fellow-worker with God. It would not make the least difference what you did, whether you prayed, whether you ever toiled or gave. God is so passionately eager that you and I, His children, should be raised up to the joy and honour of being fellow-workers with Him, that He just does not exercise the sovereignty He might—delivers His strength into captivity, limits Himself, that His children may help Him. Surely that is a motive worthy of a father— that is just the name that Jesus gives Him. You see, I don't want to be philosophical, but you might put it in another way. You might think of the purpose. Well now, if you are going to be a fellow-worker with a man, that man must have a purpose. If a man has got a purpose of building a house, every mason, every bricklayer is a fellow-worker with him. If a shipbuilder has got a purpose of building a ship, then the whole black squad, many of them ignorant men, can be fellow-workers with him. If a man has not got a purpose, you cannot be a fellow-worker with him. And it is just so with man and God. But does it ever occur to you that to have a purpose is to limit yourself? The builder would not take months to build the house if he could do it like the palace of Aladdin, all in a moment. The shipbuilder would not spend years and millions if he could create a ship just in an hour. And don't you see, if God limits Himself, if God does not in a moment complete His purposes, if God does not say in the slums of Glasgow, ' Let there be light,' as He once said in chaos, it is because He is limiting Himself to a purpose, and because only in a purpose can you and I, His children, ever be fellow-workers with Him? I have not the least doubt that the sovereign will of God could convert Africa just as we worship here ; have not the least doubt that He could change Ireland and make it in a moment the Island of the Saints, but He does not. Don't you see, if He did, you and I, His children, could never be His fellow-workers, and all the heroism and all the prayers and all the toil that has sanctified the world and made it a fit spectacle for angels to look at, all that would be just quite unknown? (I am not talking dogmatically; I am rather suggesting the kind of key that men are using to turn certain locks to-day, as they never used it before.) I think if you would only grasp that thought it might help to explain a good deal of the suffering in the world. It is the suffering of being sharers in a purpose. You take, for instance, the great French General who commanded at Verdun. Well now, why did he carry on there? Because he had the purpose of saving France. Not only he, but every man down to the commonest soldier shared in his purpose of saving France. They knew perfectly well that if wounds came, pain came, death came, all was bound up in the purpose in which they shared with their General. If God has a great purpose, and if the Lord says, 'Thy will be done,' we have got to share it, and if it is a purpose in which suffering is inevitable in such a world as this, don't you think it casts a good deal of light upon much of the suffering in the world?

Again, men are bringing this thought to bear in regard to God's creation of free beings, for if there is one thing bound up in our personality, it is the conviction we are free. I am quite certain there is nobody here this morning who, when he makes a choice, does not feel that that choice is a real choice, determined by himself. We all recognise that our battle is fixed for us by heredity, but there is not one of us but knows in his heart that his fate is in his own hands. We are free creatures. And don't you see why God made us like that ? God's purpose was love ; God wanted beings who could be in fellowship with Himself. It would be an awful thing to be a lonely God. God wanted beings who could share His purpose, think His thoughts after Him, enter into His will, pray to Him, be His children. And you could not do that unless you were free. God could easily have made us mechanical so that sin would have been impossible, so that everything we did would have been automatic. Do you think God could ever have shared His thoughts and purpose with beings like that ? Don't you see, the moment He made you free, He delivered His strength into captivity. God has created something with which He cannot interfere. The one thing God can never do, for His gifts are without repentance, is to smash and shatter your freedom by the intrusion of omnipotence. God can do just what He does in Christ—He can woo you, He can appeal to you, He can try to win you, He can give you such a beautiful example that it draws you, He can breathe His spirit on you ; but if you misuse your freedom, not even God will break in with His omnipotence to make it impossible. And yet people say, Why does God allow sin? God does not allow sin. Why does God allow the slums of Glasgow? Why did God allow the War? God never allows war. God, wanting beings to have fellowship with Him, made us free, and not even God, having made us free, can bring His omnipotence to stop us when our freewill misused gives us sin, misery, slums, the war. He cannot do it.

I am not talking dogmatically, but I just wanted to show you how men are using to-day that great scriptural thought of the self-limiting of God; when He made us free, He delivered His strength into captivity, and in that sense it is in captivity still. Without our freedom what a poor miserable thing life would be; how God would be lonely if God took all the risk. You know, I think all that is perhaps corroborated by a very deep feeling that God's children have, and that is the feeling that they can disappoint Him. Did you ever think of that? You know, when you do something that is wrong, if you are a child you disappoint your mother and your father, if you are a husband you disappoint your wife. But away deep down in every spiritual heart there is a deep feeling— and if our deepest feelings are not true I could never preach again—there is a deep feeling that

you and I can disappoint God.   My dear
brother, if your sin was predetermined from
all eternity, you could not disappoint God.
God knew about it millions of years ago, and
there could be no joy in heaven over one sinner
that repenteth.   He just, when He made us
free, delivered His strength into captivity, and
you really can disappoint Him now, you really
can give Him joy now.   That is the glory of
being free.

I will only put the thought in connection
with one other thing, just as men are doing it
to-day.   I will put the thought for a moment
in connection with Christ.   Don't you see how
it all comes to its climax, how God delivered
His strength into captivity when He gave His
only-begotten Son for you and me.   He had
done it before in regard to His sovereign will—
He had done it because He was love.   He had
done it before when He created free beings—
He had done it because He was love.   And
now, in His own way, He does it to its utmost
when He gave the Lord—He did it because
He was love.   ' God so loved the world that
He gave '—delivered Him to the captivity of
the Virgin's womb, delivered Him to the
captivity of the body that had been prepared
for Him, so that the Lord emptied Himself and
took on Him the form of a servant.   Did you

ever think — one of those undesigned co-
incidences that knit the Testaments together
—did you ever think how often the word ' delivered ' is used of the Lord Jesus Christ?
' He was delivered to the High Priest.' ' Pilate
released Barabbas and delivered Jesus.' ' He
was delivered by the counsel and foreknowledge of God.' Most beautiful of all : ' He
was delivered for our offences.' Christ was
the strength of God, and God delivered His
strength into captivity. The marvellous and
beautiful thing is just this, that by that
deliverance you and I are saved.

Will you think about that thought, will you
take it with you into the country, will you
brood on it till it becomes clear out of my very
poor and confused words, and will you remember that it is Scriptural, for this far-off writer,
illuminated by the Holy Ghost, said, ' God
delivered His strength into captivity ' ?

III

'Happy is he that hath the God of Jacob for his help.'—Ps. cxlvi. 5.

1. THE Jews seem to have found peculiar comfort, and a divine assistance not otherwise vouchsafed them, in remembering that the God they trusted in had been the guardian and guide of Jacob. There was that in God's relationship to Jacob and in Jacob's relationship to God which ministered quite peculiar consolation. That they could call on One who had brought them out of Egypt was a happy circumstance for Israel, not less happy that the God they worshipped was the great Creator of the universe ; but that a man could say when things were dark with him, ' I have the God of Jacob for my help,' seemed the happiest circumstance of all. Sometimes in reading the Life of a great man whose actions are written on the page of history we light on some tender intimate relationship that alters our whole conception of his character, and I do not think that one would err in saying that the relationship of God with Jacob profoundly altered, for every pious Jew, his conception of the character of God. It did not teach him what he had learned

already from the revelation of the world of nature. In sun, in star, in mountain and in tempest the Jew was ever alive to the eternal. But it brought him a surer comfort than the stars, cheered him more than the gladness of the sun, strengthened him when he was desolate beyond the strengthening of any hills—to remember that the God he trusted in and cried to in his human weakness was One whom he could call the God of Jacob. To have an unseen friend as Jacob had—what earthly happiness could equal that ? What message of returning spring ever could waken melody like that ? A Jew could picture no superior blessedness—nothing happier for the pilgrim-soul—than that a man through all the ways of life should have the God of Jacob for his help.

2. Probably the first encouragement afforded to one who meditated on the God of Jacob lay in the use that God had made in Jacob of very faulty and imperfect clay. There are characters in Holy Scripture that seem to be of another clay than ours. So great are they, we hardly feel in them the touch of nature that makes us all akin. In their moral and spiritual sublimity they stand remote from average humanity. They are our beacons rather than our brothers. Such was the patriarch Abraham, for example,

a man of an unequalled moral grandeur, a man whom common reverence acknowledged as worthy to be called the friend of God, a man who lived and moved and had his being on those high lawns under the eye of heaven, which few of us are privileged to visit, and fewer still are privileged to possess. Such was Moses. Who ever thinks of Moses either as a comrade or a brother ? How far away is Moses from our fellowship. What a mysterious solitude envelops him, a man in character and gift unique, consecrated to an exalted mission, dying as he had ever lived, alone. Infinite as was Israel's debt to Moses, the Psalmist does not turn to Moses' God. It does not occur to him that one is happy who hath the God of Moses for his help. For common men, fashioned of common clay that well might be the despair of any potter, he wanted another character than that.

3. Now what I suggest is that that is what he found in the relationships of God with Jacob. For if ever a man was made of faulty clay it was the patriarch who dreamed at Bethel. Not his the spiritual ardour of an Abraham ; not his the moral grandeur of a Moses ; not his that fine and beautiful material that easily takes the impress of a saint. Jacob had a coarse and

carnal nature, dogged, double, cowardly and cunning, that must have made him a terror to his neighbour and might have made him a despair to God. No one could wonder that God had chosen Abraham : that lofty soul was fit to be His friend. No one could wonder that God had chosen Isaac, with his gentle, mystic, meditative nature. The thing that thrilled the Psalmist to the deeps, and kindled hope for him when stars were darkened, was the spiritual miracle that God had wrought out of the crude material of Jacob. As if a teacher out of all his class were to set his heart on the most boorish pupil ; as if a sculptor, for his masterpiece, were to select the marble that was faultiest ; so God chose Jacob—coarse and carnal Jacob—and fashioned him into a spiritual conqueror. And the Psalmist to his dying hour never ceased to feel the wonder of it all. If there was hope for Jacob there was hope for him. If there was hope for Jacob there was hope for anybody. There was no limit to what God could do in saving and in sanctifying men. I think all that was in the Psalmist's heart when he cried out in this exultant fashion, 'Happy is he that hath the God of Jacob for his help.'

4. There come times to all of us when we quite despair of being saints. Indeed, I take it

there come times to all of us when we utterly despair of being good. The years are passing, and with the passing years we had once hoped to have been growing better, instead of which, let conscience be our witness, we are not better, rather we are worse—until it seems as if all that we had hoped for, of truth and purity and love and fellowship, were but a dream that mocked us in the morning and were destined to mock us to the end. All life's discipline has failed to sanctify us, all life's sorrow failed to make us holy, reverses have never weaned us from the world, scourgings have never brought us to our knees ; until at last how often we are tempted to yield up heavenly living in despair as if for us 'twere radically hopeless. Why speak to me about the faith of Abraham ? I am not Abraham, and never shall be. Why speak to me about the faith of Moses ? I never had it, and I never shall. My friend, I do not speak to thee of Abraham, he is as distant as the stars from thee ; but, with that brooding and despairing heart of thine, I say the God of Jacob is thy help. If there was hope for Jacob there is hope for thee. If there was heaven for Jacob there is heaven for thee. If God could choose and bless and perfect Jacob there is no limit to His redeeming grace. So in desponding and despairing hours, when character and heaven seem unattainable, all is not lost of music or of morning if one has the God of Jacob for his friend. Leave to the shining saints the God of Abraham. The God of Abraham is the praise of saints. Leave to exalted souls the God of Moses. Let them commune together on the mountain. But for tempted, faulty, worldly men and women with sinful passions and with stubborn wills, what hope is there but in the God of Jacob—One who sees the worst and hopes the best, whose darkest hour is that before the dawn, One who is merciful and very gracious and slow to anger and of great compassion, One who will cheer the heart when it is lonely, guide it through each perplexing path, grip it until the breaking of the day?

5. Another attribute of Jacob's God was His sublime and splendid perseverance, and of that the wrestling by the brook Jabbok is a parable and a witness to this hour. All night long under the stars of heaven Jacob was gripped by an unseen antagonist. It was no light conflict of a passing moment. It lasted until the breaking of the day. It told of One who having grappled with him would never leave him when the night was dark, but would hold him until the coming of the dawn. The God of Abraham

was glad in Abraham, for Abraham had responded to His call. The God of Abraham had pleasure in him and could converse with him as with a friend. But the God of Jacob many a weary year found in Jacob little cause for pleasure. He had to grip him like a wrestler in the dark. O'er moor and fen, o'er crag and torrent still He led him, and He blessed him and He kept him. He prospered him, He punished him, He guided him. He held to him and would not let him go until at last the tortuous supplanter, conquered by the persistency of heaven, laid down his arms, repented and was blessed, found in God his portion and his peace. Yes, the God of Abraham was wonderful, the God of Moses infinitely holy ; but for hard and wandering and sinful men, who is a God like to the God of Jacob, so patient, so splendidly persistent, so certain that the dawn is going to break, so confident that the best is yet to be ?

6. And we too, gathered here this morning, has ours not been the experience of Jacob ? Blessed for ever be His Holy Name, our hope and helper has been Jacob's God. Hours we have known, perchance, when God has summoned us, and then like Abraham we have obeyed the call ; and in such hours we praised

the God of Abraham, and knew Him for our
Father and our Friend. But through the years
when ways were dim and perilous, when hearts
were obdurate and hopes were failing, who has
not felt that he was saved and spared because
the God of Jacob was his help? Had he been
swift to punish our forgetfulness, who among us
would have a song this morning? Had he
despaired of us as we of heaven, long ago we
had made our bed in hell. But through the
years, the lean and wasted years, the loveless,
prayerless, and forgetful years, we have been
brought and blessed and pardoned and restored
by the infinite patience of the God of Jacob.
Lessons we would not learn He has repeated.
Duties we would not do He has forgiven.
Failures and falsehoods, rank as those of Jacob,
He has covered up in His infinite compassion.
Thus in His mercy did He deal with Jacob in
the dark backward abyss of time, thus in His
mercy is He dealing still. One may have
gained the world and yet have never found the
way of happiness. One may have health and
wealth and power and beauty, and yet may
have never found the way of happiness. But
this is certain in our so shadowy pilgrimage,
whatever a man may experience or miss—
happy is he who hath the God of Jacob for his
help. Happy at Bethel when the night is dark,

and the things of heaven seem infinitely distant ;
happy when beset by human tremblings ;
happy when the evening shadows fall ; happy
when the eyes are closed at last on the familiar
faces that we loved, to waken where partings
are no more.

IV

IN the manner of the older-fashioned Scottish preachers I want this morning to spiritualise our text, and I do not need to make any apology for desiring so to do. While I certainly believe that the primary use of this book was that it should be a series of marriage love-songs, I also believe, with many Eastern scholars, that that certainly does not exhaust the book. And, therefore, to spiritualise it and to find deeper meanings in it may have been quite in accordance with the purpose of the author. Eastern scholars can give you fifty instances in which you have got to find deeper meanings in what at first sight seemed a love-song. In the Bible of M'Cheyne, now resting in St. Peter's, Dundee, there are two bits greatly discoloured that show they were used more than any other bits, and one of them, as you would expect, is the closing chapters of St. John, and the other is the Song of Solomon. Not many of our Bibles are discoloured so to-day. A Glasgow minister of the seventeenth century, Mr.

Durham, wrote a commentary upon this book, a most admirable and feeding commentary, but the most interesting thing about the old editions to me is the list of original subscribers— Glasgow weavers, Glasgow cobblers, Glasgow maltsters, Glasgow merchants, all eager to buy a commentary on the Song of Solomon, and all of them going to feed their souls on it. To-day the book is very rarely preached on. Preaching has got its fashion. When the south wind of the spirit blows again I have not the least doubt it will come into its own. There are moods, there are ecstasies, there are close-nesses of communion with the Lord that find their truest expression in the passionate language of the Song. Well, this morning I want to take this text, and I want to spiritualise it a little, and I want to try and show you when it is that the time of the singing of birds is come. And as I want this to be a gracious sermon I will try and put it all in terms of grace, the grace of the Lord Jesus Christ.

Well now, first, the literal time of the singing of birds comes when grace makes beautiful the face of nature. You see the flowers appear upon the earth, and the flowers are just emblems of God's grace. That is always how the Master looked on them. I suppose all of you know the difference between love and grace. Grace is love that stoops. Love radiates in every direction—grace radiates downwards. Love is between equal and equal or between inferior and superior ; grace, may I say, grace is love toward the bottom dog. It was grace that brought our Saviour down, we know the grace of the Lord Jesus ; it is grace that brings the Holy Spirit here, He is the spirit of grace as well as of supplication ; and when the grace of God, the stooping love of God, makes all nature beautiful in summer, then the time of the singing of birds is come. Of course there are birds that sing in winter. December is not altogether silent ; there are touches of melody for the hearing ear even when the snow is on the ground ; but the full choir, the vocal forest, the blending of ten thousand harmonies—that only comes when grace is beautiful upon the face of nature. Then the nightingale begins in England, then the thrush begins in Scotland—there is a thrush that sings here upon the Sunday evenings as if it just wanted to worship God—and then the lark, as Mr. Spurgeon says, ' does what we all should do, mounts heavenward singing as it mounts.' Yes, when grace makes beautiful the face of nature, in a literal sense the time of the singing of birds is come.

But now, don't you see, not only is that true,

but it is also true when grace is poured upon the Church. Gracious times are always singing times. I read in Friday's evening paper about an English landlord who wanted to eject his tenant, and his reason for wanting to eject him was that the man had got converted in the Salvation Army. But it was not his conversion he objected to, it was this, that the man had started singing, and morning, noon, and evening he was singing. I have great sympathy with that landlord, and landlords do not get much sympathy to-day. The point is that always down the ages gracious times have been singing times, from the hour when the angels sang above Bethlehem to the hour of that ejected lodger, and the song has been the secret of victory. There is a play by Ibsen called *The Emperor Julian*, and in the play there is a Christian called Apollinaris, and Apollinaris says a very glorious thing when the beast has got its claws into the Church. He says, 'Verily I say unto you, so long as song rings out above our suffering, the beast is going to be defeated.' That is perfectly true. Gracious times are always singing times, gracious epochs in the Church are always musical. When the sword of the Lord is in the Church's hand, the song of the Lord is on the Church's lips. When grace is outpoured on the Church, the time of the singing of birds is come.

Well now, if you ask me to illustrate that, suppose we send our thoughts first to the time of Pentecost, and I take Pentecost because this is Whit Sunday, and the Church Universal is thinking back to that. They were all filled with the Holy Ghost then ; when Peter preached thousands were converted ; lives were changed down to the very deeps. The change showed itself in fifty ways, but I am certain that what impressed the multitude was that morning, noon, and evening these Pentecostal believers were praising God. Look at it in that second chapter. Do you remember when Paul writes to the Corinthians, he gives advice especially about prayer and singing, as if the outpouring of the Holy Spirit showed itself specially in prayer and singing? No Methodist meeting was ever so rapturous as these Pentecostal meetings, and Paul with his majestic statesmanship felt himself bound to guide them. Then the very earliest notice which we have of Christian worship comes from a charming pen, the pen of Pliny, who was asked by his Emperor to try and discover what it was that Christians did at worship. Pliny was in Asia Minor, and writes to his Emperor that he had discovered it. He says, ' They meet at daybreak to sing hymns to Christ as God.' Everywhere singing, at home and in the street, at midnight, in the chill hour of daybreak when you don't feel like singing, these Pentecostal men, filled with the Spirit, everywhere praising God. Don't you see, the Spirit was poured out upon the Church, and the time of the singing of birds was come ?

And not only is that true of Pentecost, it is also true of the Reformation. The Reformation sang itself to victory, as Cromwell did at the battle of Dunbar. You will never understand the Reformation unless you remember it is a spiritual movement ; it used politics and it used statesmanship, but at its heart it was neither. It was the outpouring of the Spirit of God, leading men to break through every barrier and to get freedom of access to Himself ; it was the hunger of the human heart, it was the thirst of the human soul, it was the child weary of being excluded, clamouring for access to its Father, and the notable thing is that everywhere not only was there suffering and perils, but everywhere throughout Europe there was song. The Reformation sang itself to victory. The hymns of Luther were like battle-cries ; in Scotland *The Good and Godly Ballads*, as the book was called, went hand in hand with the preaching of John Knox. Men sang them as they followed the plough, women sang them as they rocked the cradle, fishermen sang them when they shot their nets, and decent people who were fast asleep by the time that Knox reached his tenth or fifteenth, were brought to Christ, brought into the Light, by the singing of the Good and Godly Ballads. You see, grace was poured upon the Church, the doctrines of grace hidden in mediæval past came to the front again, the gracious person of the Lord threw off its veil and was seen by the common people, and strangely, when grace was poured upon the Church, the time of the singing of birds was come.

But not only was it true of the Reformation ; is not it true of every revival—every revival time is a singing time ? You have John Wesley going out to preach : you have Charles Wesley, his brother, writing his beautiful hymns. You have Mr. Moody coming to Scotland : you have got Mr. Sankey by his side. We are so accustomed to it we never think of it, but I never heard of any Mohammedan missionary— some of them are just as devout as ours—I never heard of any Buddhist missionary who ever did anything like that.

My senior colleague in Thurso, Dr. Taylor, ordained by Edward Irving in 1829, was sent over as a deputy to Ireland to the great revival

of the later 'fifties, and he often in old days
used to talk to me about the wonderful things
he had seen there and about all that it meant
to his own soul. There was one thing that
struck me ; it was this. He very seldom talked
about the preaching, but what he loved to talk
of was the hymns, and especially one hymn,
' What 's the news ? ' You know we never sang
hymns in Thurso. We sang psalms, and sang
them sitting ; even paraphrases were innovations. You see, fifty years had gone since that
revival, and he had forgotten almost all the
preaching, but he had never forgotten the thrill
and throb and pulse of these revival hymns.
And then, for he had known M'Cheyne, and
he was steeped in the language of this book, he
would say sometimes, ' Yes, the winter was
past, the flowers appeared on the earth, and
the time of the singing of birds was come.'

Will you please notice how my thought goes.
First, it comes when grace is beautiful upon
the face of nature ; second, it comes when
grace is poured out upon the Church ; and
now will you please take this, it comes when
grace leads any man to full surrender. Will
you notice the opening words of our text,
' Arise, my love, my fair one, and come away.'
Just the Bridegroom speaking to the soul,
calling us away from all our beastly things and

half-heartedness and worldliness, and calling
us in love, ' Arise, my love, and come away.'
And then, the moment that you do that, the
time of the singing of birds is come. That
is always true. I should like to illustrate it
from another text in the Old Testament. It is
a great text, though you may never have
noticed it. Great texts are like great men,
they are not half so visible as lesser people.
The text is in the Second Book of Chronicles
(of all books !), 29th chapter, 27th verse, where
we read about Hezekiah and how he reformed
the temple worship, and then, talking about
burnt-offering, the text says, ' When the burnt-
offering began, the song of the Lord began
also.' If you don't feel the touch of God in that,
in Chronicles, mark you, if you don't feel it to
be a parable of life, I think things are hopeless
with your vision. What was the burnt-
offering ? Something entirely different from
the sin - offering. The burnt-offering, the
offering of surrender, of yielding yourself to
God ; and the moment the burnt-offering
begins, a kind of parable of your surrender,
the song of the Lord began also. Do I speak
to any here this morning who are holding back
from full surrender, and holding back just
because they are afraid that the song and
music of life would have to go ? It is an

egregious mistake. Selfishness always becomes silent ; self-surrender is the road to singing. Why, is not it so in daily life ? Must not you be whole-hearted if you are going to sing at work ? Did you ever hear any man singing at his work who was half-hearted and a slacker ? In all my long experience I never recall a time when there was so much singing as during the Great War, and then men surrendered everything ; they surrendered everything to duty, laid the burnt-offering upon the altar, surrendered wife, surrendered child, surrendered mother, surrendered home, and in the camp and on the railway train and on the march and in the troopship, such singing as one never heard before. Yield yourself to Him, give yourself up in glad surrender, hear the Bridegroom say to you this morning, ' Rise up, my love, and come away,' and the moment that you do it the time of the singing of birds is come.

I hope you have followed my line of thought. It comes when grace is beautiful on the face of nature, it comes when grace is poured on the Church, it comes when grace leads any man to self-surrender. And now, lastly, in a word, it comes when grace is perfected in glory. There are all the trumpets on the other side. In Upper Egypt ' where the spreading Nile,' as

the poet says, 'parts hundred-gated Thebes'—
in Upper Egypt there stood, and for all I know
may still stand, a statue known as that of
Memnon. You remember the statue of Memnon was one of the Seven Wonders of the
World : and it was that not because it was
beautiful, not because it was colossal, but
because every morning when the sun rose and
the first beams of the sun smote upon the statue,
from its brazen lips there came out music. And
so you and I are going to have our morning,
' the summer morn I 've sighed for,' as the
hymn says, in a brighter and a better world than
this, where sorrow and sighing shall have fled
away. And wherever heaven is, in whatever
unimaginable region of God's universe, one
thing you are certain of : that is, it is going to
be a state of song ; going to be that because
it is all of grace, because we will never get to
heaven by our deserts ; going to be that
because music can express what the subtlest
speech never can express. 'I think I should
have no moral wants,' said Maggie Tulliver
in that charming story, *The Mill on the Floss*,
' if I had only enough music.' Well, Maggie,
you are going to get it by and by. We are so
apt to think of death as a grim hand rushing
us to the darkness, and death is not that at all.
Death is the Bridegroom, saying, ' Rise up, my

love, my fair one, and come away ; for the winter is past, the rains are over, again flowers appear on the earth.' And when grace is perfected in glory, the time of the singing of birds is come.

V

'Why sayest thou, O Jacob, and speakest, O Israel, My way is hid from the Lord, and my judgment is passed over from my God?'—Isaiah xl. 27.

You have got to remember that these words were spoken by Israel in exile. They had been carried away from their own land, and they were captives in the land of Babylon. To a degree that we can hardly understand, God and land were connected in antiquity. A nation could suffer almost any punishment so long as it was living in its country, but whenever they were driven away, as Israel had been driven away to Babylon, they at once thought that God had forgotten to be gracious. You see, it was not that they were badly treated in Babylon, because the evidence is all the other way. No doubt they were allowed to build their synagogues and possibly to traffic in the market. But the thing that moved them to their deeps was this, that God seemed to have forgotten all about them, that He had forgotten to be gracious. And so they hung their harps upon the willow trees, and they sat down by the Babylonian water-courses, and with dreary eyes they looked at one another, and they said, ' My way is hid from the Lord, and my judgment is passed over from my God.'

I think there are two thoughts you have got to bear in mind if you want to understand how utter was their desolation, and the first is the great thought of the exodus. You know the great hour in Israel's history was when God delivered them from Egypt, took them from the house of bondage, carried them to the Promised Land ; and the very glory of the exodus was just this, that they were under the leadership of God. Every morning when they wakened, there before them was the pillar of cloud. Every night when they went to rest, there burning was the pillar of fire. Every month, every week, every hour, from the time of Egypt to the Promised Land, they were under the leadership of Heaven, and cannot you understand the awful desolation when that leadership was taken away? They were like travellers in the Alps who had been conducted by the best of guides, and one morning they would waken, and precipices are all around them, and in the night the guide has stolen away. (I don't say it was so, but I do say that is what they felt.) Again, if you want to understand their utter desolation, you have got to think of the names they give to God here. They call Him ' Lord,' that is, ' Jehovah ' ;

and then they say ' My God.' You know,
' Jehovah' was a peculiar name ; no other
nation had the right to use it. It was revealed
first to Moses ; it was strong with tender
memories. And not only was He ' Jehovah '
their own, their covenant God, but He was
' My God,' and He had left them. If a little
child were travelling with a casual stranger,
and the casual stranger disappeared, the little
child might cry, but it would not really be
broken-hearted. But if the little child said,
' The woman who has left me is my mother,'
don't you see it would be broken-hearted ?
And Israel cried out, ' He is my God.' What
I want you to feel is, it was a dark spiritual
desolation. It was not that they were hardly
treated, it was not even that they were far
away from home. The awful agony of the
exile to people so spiritual as the Jews was this,
' My way is hid from the Lord, and my judgment is passed over from my God.' You know,
that is not only the cry of history, that is also
a cry of the human heart. The wonderful thing
about the heart is this, that when you get deep
enough it is always one. Why, the tears that
flowed ten thousand years ago are just the tears
that flow this morning. The smile that
brightened things ten thousand years ago is
just the smile that brightens things to-day.

Let a mother be glad over her little child—
could a mother rise of twenty centuries ago she
would understand the brightness of your glance.
That is why we need a changeless Saviour, the
same yesterday, to-day, and for ever ; just
because the heart He comes to save is the same
yesterday, to-day, and for ever. And, you
know, that is a great mark of the inspiration
of the Bible, that out of a little bit of ancient
history it can wrest and wring the universal
element. Don't you think these Israelites said
a great deal more than this ? but that was
ephemeral, nugatory, transient, of no per-
manent value, and it is lost in the oblivion of
time. But they uttered one cry that is just as
true to-day as it was when they uttered it, and
God has preserved that. That is a mark, you
who are tempted to think lightly of the Old
Testament, of the inspiration of God's Word,
that all the rest has gone down the stream of
time, and the one cry from these Babylonian
saints that is echoed in every human heart is
preserved for us in the Word.

I wonder what the reasons are that tempt
people to cry this cry to-day. I am not just
here to talk about the Christ of history ; I want
to get to the secret of your hearts ; and I
wonder if you would think with me for a few
moments while we consider why it is to-day

that all of us are tempted to say, ' My way is hid from the Lord.' I think, firstly, many people are tempted that way now, just because of the vastness of our universe. (Earl Balfour was talking about that on Friday.) You know to the Psalmist the world in which he lived was the centre of all created things, and above the world there was the heaven, and not very far beyond it was the Throne of God. And of course, if you believe that, it is very easy to think that God is watching you, and that you are of tremendous importance in His sight. But, thanks to our modern knowledge, the earth has been cast out of its centrality ; it is a little insignificant planet, one of a million bigger than itself ; it is of no more value than a grain of sand. And if you grasp that, and you ought to grasp it, for you are not here to be blind to modern knowledge, is not it sometimes very easy to say, ' My way is hid from the Lord, and my judgment is passed over from my God ' ? And the awful thing is, that when you say it, life becomes incredibly difficult ; it takes away the spirit from a man. Nevermore can you be absolutely certain that your cup is plenished by a hand of love. Nevermore can you be absolutely certain that guidance and not chance is at the back of you. Nevermore can you face death as just an instant opening on to a fuller life. You have got to reckon with the two alternatives.

And then, are we not very often tempted to say that just by the bitter disappointments of our life ? You find that in the Bible constantly ; and please remember this, that whenever you find anything in the Bible over and over again, that means that it is common to the human heart. Well now, you think of Job. Job was a bitterly disappointed man. Job had sought to serve God with a perfect heart ; he had looked for the reward of virtue, and here he was sitting in the ashes. And the whole temptation of the Book of Job, if you read it, is just this, ' My way is hid from the Lord, and my judgment is passed over from my God.' Or, again, take the Baptist when he was in prison. The Baptist was a bitterly disappointed man. The Baptist had looked for Christ with His axe and with His fan, and here was a meek and lowly Saviour, and in the bitterness of his disappoint-ment this was his temptation, to echo the cry of the exiles in Babylon. Or once again, don't you read in Second Peter, the people were look-ing for the coming of the Lord ; every morning they expected Him ; they said, ' The Lord is coming to-day ' ! And when the months went on and the Lord did not come, they were bitterly disappointed, and what they said was

just the cry, ' My way is hid from the Lord.'
And it is just so this morning. When somebody
we trust disappoints us, when some plan we
have raised becomes a house of cards, when
some prize we strove for somebody else gets,
when illness interrupts our work, when the
chair is empty and the grave is full, are not we
tempted yet to.cry, although perhaps we never
do it openly, ' My way is hid from the Lord,
and my judgment is passed over from my
God ' ?

Again, just to change the thought a little,
are not we tempted, you and I, to say it when
our sin seems to go unpunished ? Is there anybody sitting here who is cherishing the sweet
thought that they have sinned and are not
going to be punished ? You know, the Bible
comes to you and says, sin is always punished—
' As a man soweth, so shall he also reap ' ; and
you sit and you recall the sin this moment, and
you know you have never been punished yet.
I would not be surprised if, like a sweet morsel
under your tongue, you are rolling this thought,
I am an exception ; my way is hid from the
Lord, and my judgment is passed over from
my God. In this mysterious world there are
not many things we can be sure of. We certainly cannot be sure of to-morrow, for we
know not what an hour may bring forth. But

there is one thing you may be sure of, with all
the authority and majesty of God, and that is,
' Be sure your sin will find you out.' Mark you,
the Scripture does not say, ' Be sure your sin
will be found out.' The Scripture is always
true to fact, and that is not a fact. A man may
die with his sin a secret ; but what the Scripture says is this, ' Be sure your sin will find *you*
out,' and that is always and everywhere the
truth. It finds you out in the hardening of
heart, it finds you out in the chilling of your
judgment, it finds you out in the dimming of
your vision, it finds you out in the hardening
of your feelings, it finds you out in the lessening
of your influence. There are men here who are
saying, ' Well, I have sinned, but, thank God,
my influence is just as great as ever.' And they
did not know, what everybody else knows, that
their influence is weakening every day. It finds
you out sometimes in the dearest of all places,
in your children, and your children's children.
If there is anybody here this morning who,
having sinned, is rolling it like a sweet morsel
under his tongue, ' My way is hid from the
Lord, and my judgment is passed over from my
God,' stop and say, ' Father, I have sinned, and
am no more worthy to be called Thy child ' ;
and ' though your sins be as scarlet they shall
be white as snow ; though they be red like

crimson they shall be as wool'; and now, this
very moment, while we are sitting here.

I think sometimes, and now I am talking to
the saints of God, I think sometimes we are
tempted to say this when we experience delays
in prayer. You know there is nothing so trying
to a man's faith as just to be delayed in the
answers to his prayers. Thomas Boston of
Ettrick, that sweet saint whose name makes
fragrant the valleys of the south, in his diary
says frequently, ' Got my studies over and so
went to prayer, because I have a suit pending
before God.' Don't you see, years before he
had begun praying for something, and it was
like a suit pending before God, and he was
praying still. I wonder how many of us have
got faith like that? Don't you think when
Martha and Mary sent for Christ, when to-
morrow morning came He was not there, when
evening fell and there was no sound of His foot-
step, don't you think that Martha would look
to Mary and say, ' Mary, our way is hid from
the Lord, and our judgment is passed over
from our God '? And that is why Christ tells
us insistently that we are never to faint in
prayer. When we pray for light and we do not
get light ; when we are only plunged into a
deeper darkness ; when we pray for strength
against our besetting sin, and the next tempta-

tion unhorses us, and there we are, supine in
the dust ; when we pray for a blessing for some
dear one, and the years go on and it never
seems to come, are we not tempted, just like
the exiles by the water-courses in Babylon, to
say, ' My way is hid from the Lord ' ? There
is a very true sense in which the whole of
Scripture is just an answer to that temptation ;
but I think if you study the Scripture you will
discover that there are three great arguments
that Scripture uses to men like us, in that condition. Will you allow me a moment, while I
tell you what they are. There is, first of all,
the argument from nature. You will observe
that that is the prophet's argument. He says,
' Lift up your eyes on high and behold who
hath created these things,' and ' these things '
are the stars. ' He calleth *them* (put the
emphasis on ' them ') all by names by the
greatness of His might, for that He is strong in
power not one faileth.' You have got to
picture the prophet sitting amid the Jews on
the sands of Babylon, and above them the
glittering stars of the Eastern night, and he says,
' Children, if God names every one of these, if
God makes their rising and their setting, do
you think your way is hid from Him ? ' You
see it is the argument of the prophet, it is the
argument of Jesus ; only Jesus does not bid

you look up, He bids you look down. He
does not say, 'Look up at the stars.' He
says, 'Look down at that little flower at your
feet.'

And then it is also the argument of poetry :

'Confide ye aye in Providence, for Providence
    is kind,
And bear ye a' life's changes with a calm and
    tranquil mind,
Tho' pressed and hemm'd on every side, hae
    faith and ye'll win thro',
For ilka blade o' grass keps its ain drap
    o' dew.'

Men tell us in their superior way that our
modern knowledge of nature has exploded that
argument, but when it comes to a matter of the
soul I take sides with the prophet, with the poet,
and with Christ.

And then will you remember that there is
the great argument of history, and the true
reason why histories are in the Bible is not to
give subjects for historical criticism (the men
who wrote them were not thinking of the
higher critics) ; the very object of histories in
the Bible is to enable you and me to say, when
everything is dark, 'Thank God, I can trust in
Him.' You think of Joseph. When Joseph
was carried down to Egypt, away from his

father and his home, heart-broken, bound in the caravan for a strange country, don't you think Joseph was crying, ' My way is hid from Jehovah ' ? and yet you have the story. Joseph was in the lap of God, Joseph was on the way to honour and to his crown. You think of Jonah—just the same. You think of Paul. You know there came a day in Paul's life when he wanted to get into Bithynia and could not, and he wanted to get into Mysia and he could not, and the only road open was by the sea, and like a true Jew, Paul hated the sea. And I suppose he was saying, ' My way is hid from the Lord, and my judgment is passed over from my God ' ; and he was on the way to Europe, and he was on the way to the evangelisation of the world, and you and I in Scotland can sing, ' I 'll bless the hand that guided, I 'll bless the heart that planned.' Every history written in the Bible is not written there to be the sport of critics. Every history written in the Bible is written for its moral ends, and the great end of all of them is this, that when it is dark, when every star is dim, when your heart is empty and is aching, you can never say again, never, ' My way is hid from the Lord.'

And then there is the third argument, and, of course, that is the argument of Christ, and it is the quiet utterance of these words, ' He that hath seen Me hath seen the Father.' When you think how our blessed Saviour kept His eye upon the one, a poor woman, of no value, no social standing at all ; when you think how He traced the one, followed Peter through all his circuitings and windings, and then when you quietly say, ' He that hath seen Me hath seen the Father,' however you may be tempted, however difficult life has been, however hard it is to think you and yours are in the hands of love, if you are faithful, you will never say again, ' My way is hid from the Lord, and my judgment is passed over from my God.'

VI

'Then was Jesus led up of the Spirit into the wilderness to be tempted of the devil.'—Matt. iv. 1.

IF our blessed Saviour had to be the very Son of Man, it was, of course, inevitable that He should be tempted, because that is the one experience nobody ever escapes ; it is the touch of nature—one of the touches of nature—that makes us all akin. A man may escape great calamity, a man may escape overpowering illness, a man may escape the perils of being very poor and the perils of being very rich ; but there is one thing that nobody escapes, from the king on his throne to the beggar on the highway, that is, the experience of being tempted. And therefore, if our Lord was to be the perfect Son of Man, it was quite inevitable He should be tempted. The man who is never tempted has either sunk to the level of the beast, or risen to the level of angels. Is there anybody here this morning who is never tempted now, just because evil has got a right-of-way across him ? anybody who can do things this morning with unconcern that twenty years ago would have made him halt a

moment ? I don't think there is any prayer for
such a man except just, ' Lord, create a clean
heart within me, and renew within me a right
spirit.' Of course, if we were all tempted on
our worst side, our blessed Saviour could never
have been tempted, because all His gates
opened on to heaven—some of yours and mine
open on to hell. But I think you will see how,
in our common life, we are very often tempted
not on the side of what is bad, but just on the
side of what is good. Here is a mother, and
how she loves her son ; it is the finest thing
about her. She used to be a careless girl, and
now she is a self-sacrificing woman. How
often mothers are just tempted not on the side
of what is bad, but just in that beautiful love
for her dear son. Or here is a man very, very
fond of his wife and children—some one once
said that whenever the devil tempts an Englishman he always does it in the guise of wife and
children—here is a man very fond of his wife
and children ; it is the most beautiful thing
about him ; in business he has got rather a
shady character, but he is almost perfect in
his home. How often a man is tempted, perhaps, just to do things that conscience does not
agree to because of his dear care for wife and
children. You see, you and I are very often
tempted not on the side of what is bad, but on

the side of what is good ; and if you follow out that thought a little, don't you come to see it was possible that our Lord was tempted, and all His gates opening on to heaven ? I think sometimes we are very apt to misconceive the sinlessness of Christ, as if it was a garment given to Him by God, and He could not put it off even if He tried. It was not a garment, it was a victory. It was not an endowment, it was an achievement. Every hour the Lord was tempted, and every hour He put it from Him, until at last His sinlessness was final, and He cried, ' It is finished.' And if you regard that as the sinlessness of Jesus, wrought out every moment, every moment tempted, every moment obedient to God until the end, you begin to see He was tempted just as you and I are.

The thought I wanted to follow out this morning was this. I wanted to ask, Along what lines did the tempter come to Christ ? because if we discover that, then we begin to understand that He was tempted just as we are. You know it is very difficult to feel that Christ is just our brother. There is so much in Him that is different—His power, His nature is so unlike yours and mine, that it is a kind of relief to discover a touch of brotherhood. That is why we love to hear that He was weary— perhaps some of you are weary now ; that is

why we love to hear that He was hungry —
there are people even in this audience that
have known hunger ; that is why we love to
hear that He was tempted—it draws Him near
us. And if we discover the tempter came to
Him very much as he comes to you and me,
you have got a brother born for adversity.
There is nothing in life like that.

I want you to note, first, how the tempter
came to Him at the very beginning of His task,
before He had wrought a single miracle, before
He had said a single word. I suppose that in
these forty days in the wilderness our Lord was
meditating on the future. I don't think there
was a single incident that ever came to Him
that our Lord had not anticipated in these
forty days. He was looking forward to all that
was coming, and it was just then the devil
tempted Him. I think there are three times
in every great task when a man is peculiarly
liable to be tempted. The first is the start,
when things are looming up before you. The
second is when you are halfway through, the
arrow that flieth at midday, when you have
lost the glow and glory of the morning. The
third is at the end, when you are tempted
to think it has all been just a failure : like
Lord Kelvin across the way : near the end of
his career he said he could only describe his

life as a failure. I think it would be easy to show that our Lord was tempted at these times —right in the middle when the first enthusiasm had died away, right at the end when He had to turn to Peter and say, ' Get thee behind Me, Satan,' and here, just at the beginning. There is a curious correspondence in many details at the end of His life with the details of the start, and I sometimes think that out in the desert here there had been something of Gethsemane, ' Father, if it be possible, let this cup pass from Me.' It was going to be an awful cup, awful, bitter as gall. And then, just in an instant, ' Nevertheless not what I will, but what Thou wilt.'

Just at the start our blessed Lord was tempted. There may be some one here this morning who is starting a new task, perhaps in the Church, perhaps in the city, called to it by your duty. Well, if you are a light-weight, one of these jaunty people, of course it won't trouble you. My experience is that these kind of jaunty people never get there. But if you are deep and serious, and take life earnestly, when the thing looms up before you, you are tempted to despair. I remember an eminent man in this city, called to a great task, telling me how the first thing he did (he was not commonly afraid) was to bow his head down in his hands and say to a friend, ' It can't be done.' Whenever you have these temptations, is not it a great thing that you are sure the Lord knows it ? He has been there. He understands ; you can get His fellowship even in that. A young writer once wrote to Sir Walter Scott, and he said, ' Sir, I don't know how it is, but just when I am beginning a new book my heart sinks, formless fears surge up.' And Scott, that gallant heart, wrote back, ' My dear fellow, I feel it just as much as you do.' You have got to think how that young writer was encouraged by the sympathy of that great soul, and you and I have got the sympathy of some one infinitely greater.

Or again, somebody is here this morning who is starting a far more difficult task, and that is the task of taking up your cross, the task of bearing a great sorrow. By and by it will get a little easier. Time is a great healer ; time rubs the edges off the boldest granite on the Arran hills. Men picture time with a scythe ; I picture time with a vial of balm that it just pours into your gaping wounds. But at the very outset, is not it difficult ? A few weeks ago, a month ago, you lost somebody very dear ; now you are called to a task that is going to last through life ; that is, bearing your cross of sorrow. At the very beginning are not you tempted, tempted to wonder if God is love, tempted to wonder if God cares, tempted to be dull and heartless when other lives are dependent on your brightness? It is a great thing to think that in an hour of that kind you have the sympathy, the understanding of the Lord Jesus. His task was not to manage a business. His task was to bear a cross : ' Was ever sorrow like unto My sorrow ? ' And at the very start, to Him, just as to you, comes the devil, tempting you to doubt the Father, and to wonder if there is any love in heaven. ' In every pang that rends the heart, the Man of Sorrows had a part.'

Again, I think it must occur to you that our Lord was tempted in the hour of reaction. I suppose you all know what reaction is ? It is the recoil after a time of stress and excitement. Our Lord was subtly tempted in the hour of reaction. Well now, consider. I suppose the hour of the baptism of Christ, which just pre-ceded, was an hour of the most terrific strain. You have got to try and picture it. It lies there quietly upon the Gospel page, but when you get to its meaning what an hour of strain it was—the old now gone, the quiet and beauty of Nazareth, the love of His mother. ' Woman, what have I to do with thee ? ' was just coming, and then all the future of blood and sorrow, and all that; the cleavage of it, the baptism, and then identified with sinful man, and then equipped by the Holy Ghost for all His ministry, and then heaven opening and a voice speaking to Him—try and think of the tremendous strain of it. Mark tells us that He was driven to the wilderness. I wonder no great painter has ever painted that. The Lord bowed and driven by what was uncontrollable to get alone to think it all out, and then for forty days so wrapped in it that He quite forgot to eat. And then, suddenly, spent in every power, and wearied to His finger-tips, *then* the devil comes—is not he subtle? Then the devil comes, in the very hour of reaction. Not when the candle of God is shining on His head, not when all the lights are burning, not when He is strong and quivering with life, but in that awful hour of weakness and reaction. Brother, sister, is not it so still? The devil leaves us when we are happy, and comes back when the tide is at the ebb. I want you to remember in these hours when there is no music, when all the lights are burning dim, when you are so weary you can hardly face your task, when after some time of spiritual intensity you are tempted, that the Lord knows it. He was just so tempted, He has just come through it. He holds out His hand and calls you brother.

There is only one thing more I want to say, and it is this. I want you to notice how our Lord was tempted along the line of His desires, along the line of His ambitions (if I might venture to use that somewhat degraded word). You have that in every one of the temptations ; you have it specially in the third. He would go out and preach about the Kingdom—no man worth anything preaches on what he has not given his intense thought to when you were busy at your business—and the Lord had been thinking of the Kingdom in these forty days when He was all alone, I suppose, saying to Himself, ' My mother thought the Kingdom was for the Jews, and God, My Father, is show-ing Me that it is not. The Kingdom is going to include every kingdom in the world.' And just then the devil comes to Him, and what does he do ? Contradict Him ? Never ! The devil comes and says, ' Sir, that is a most laud-able ambition ; accept my help ; just let me give you a hand on, and all the kingdoms of the world will become yours.' And our Lord said, ' Get thee behind Me, Satan.' You understand, taken on the line of His desires. That is exactly what happens to-day. You think, for instance, of a preacher. Well now, that preacher is on fire to preach the Gospel, but what is the use of preaching when the

church is empty ?   Of course, his deep desire,
though he does not say it to you, is to have his
church full.   And just then the devil comes
to him and—contradicts him? Never. Says,
That is a poor kind of ambition ?   Nothing of
the kind.   The devil says, ' Now I want you to
let me help you.   Don't preach on such and
such things ; be modern, just avoid the Cross ;
sometimes take a risky subject about the eternal
triangle ; advertise flaming, flashing titles, just
have a touch of the music-hall about your
service, and it will all come right.'   And the
Lord says, ' Get thee behind Me, Satan.'

You have got a man whose great ambition
is to get on, and, mark you, he could scarcely
have a better.   Men who are content to be
failures are not in God's line.   Here is a man
determined to get on, wanting to get on—and
he is perfectly right, and the more of you who
get on the better.   And then Satan comes to
him.   Does he contradict him?   Does he say
to him, 'Friend, you ought to have higher
motives than that'?   He says, 'Won't you just
allow me to help you a little ? '   The man is
tempted to do something that he knows is
wrong.   The man is tempted to give bribes ;
to say, Of course everybody gives them, and I
have my wife and children to look after.   And
the Lord was tempted just like that, and the

Lord said, ' Get thee behind Me, Satan.' The point is, are you a follower of His ? It all comes to that. If you are not, you can do what you like. But what right have you to call yourself a disciple of Christ if in such hours you accept such help as that ? None, no more than I would have as a preacher if I advertised flashy titles and had Scotch songs sung here on my platform. Here is a man who is given to writing books, as so many people have an itch to do. Suppose he wants to be famous, and that is perfectly right. ' Fame is the last infirmity of noble minds,' says Milton. Mark you, of *noble* minds. Then the devil comes to him, never contradicts, says, ' Friend, I want to help you to have your name on every lip,' and tells him the sort of book to write—several of the Commandments broken, and yet everything coming right. I need not dwell on that. But the point is that the Lord says, ' Get thee behind Me, Satan.' The singular thing is this, that when the Lord took the long, slow, bloody way, there came into His heart a joy and peace that the world could never give, and has never taken away. And there is coming to Him a triumph ten thousand times greater than if He accepted the advice of Satan :

> ' Jesus shall reign where'er the sun
> Does his successive journeys run.'

VII

*' When the Son of Man shall come in His glory,
and all the holy angels with Him, then shall He sit
on the throne of His glory.'*—Matthew xxv. 31.

ONE always notices in time of revival that a
great deal is preached about the Last Judgment. In our ordinary pulpit ministration
it is not so. I think most ministers hesitate to
face up to these awful truths, but always, both
in past centuries and to-day, when there is a
revival of God's Spirit, as a moral motive
power you find prominence on the Last Judgment. Over against the inequalities, the in-
justices, the apparent unrighteousnesses of this
world, mankind almost naturally has postulated
a judgment to come. I suppose there is not a
savage faith without some glimmering of it ;
and in the religion of old Egypt there was no
picture more familiar than that of the Judgment Hall, and somebody standing holding a
pair of scales, and in one side of them the
human souls.

One wants, then, to find what our Lord had
to say about this deep instinct of the human
heart. We find it here. Laying aside the
imagery—one can never be quite sure when or

not the curtain is the picture—but trying to lay aside the imagery and trying to get at the truth which our Lord wanted to teach, I think we discover this. First of all, our Lord makes it perfectly plain to us that this judgment is going to be at the end of time ; when the Son of Man cometh in His glory and His holy angels with Him, *then*—and whatever be our thoughts of eschatology, and whatever be our views of the millennium, I think it must be clear to all of us that what our Lord meant was that the great judgment is not to be until the story of time is at an end. Now a little reasoning will just show you how necessary that is. For instance, nobody can be perfectly judged in this life, just because life is not static ; life is a thing of movement. Our blessed Lord never judged a man by what he might be at the particular moment, but rather by the trend of what he was going to be. You take the parable of the Pharisee and Publican praying in the Temple. At that particular moment the Pharisee was really a better man than the Publican, he had done far more good, but in the broken heart of the poor penitent the Lord saw such possibilities for to-morrow that He pronounced blessing on his head. You take a man like John Newton, who was a friend of Cowper. I suppose many of you know that in his earlier years John Newton was a slave-trader, and if at any hour in his earlier life you had judged him you would have condemned him to the lowest pit. But Newton was converted, Newton became a well-known minister, Newton won multitudes of souls for Christ. You see, you can never judge him while his life is moving. Again, is it not equally clear to you that you can never judge a man just when he dies, because when a man dies his influence does not die; it may go on from age to age. You take, for instance, a case like Mr. Quarrier. Mr. Quarrier with all the passion of his heart loved these little orphan children, and then he got the Homes built at Bridge-of-Weir, and there he laboured till he died; but the Homes did not die. Year after year, generation after generation, perhaps to the end of time, they are going to go on blessing the orphan children. If you want to sum up the total influence of Mr. Quarrier you cannot judge him till the end of time. You take a man whose influence is bad: a man who writes a bad book, it may be an obscene novel, spawn of the press, it may be a book deliberately designed to overthrow faith. The man writes it and gets his bread by it, and he dies; but the book does not die. Year after year it may go on corrupting, degrading, and lowering, and not till the ripples have broken on the shore of eternity is the whole story of the man's influence known, and our Lord, who is always so reasonable, says that when the Son of Man comes, when time is done, when your influence has gone to its uttermost limit, *then* we are going to be judged.

The next thing our Lord tells us here is that the judgment is going to be final. I want you to listen while I read over quietly these words— not of mine, but of Christ : ' And these shall go away into everlasting punishment, and the righteous unto life eternal.' If there be anybody here who knows Greek, he will know that the word for ' everlasting ' is the same word as the word for ' eternal,' and therefore if you and I believe that the life we are going to live beyond is one that never ends, you can only interpret the words of Christ as meaning that the punishment is never going to end. I want you to think of that. It is perfectly true that men have tried to get out of it by giving another meaning to that word ' eternal.' They have taken it to mean ' age-long ' : that is, lasting through the next period to this, though beyond that no one knows what happens. There is no hope that way. All through the Bible—St. Paul, St. John, the writer of the Hebrews, the Revelation—the word means ' never ending.' So it means in classic Greek, so it means in

Plato. It is not I, it is the Lord who says, and
says it with a passionate intensity, ' Where the
worm never dieth, where the fire is never
quenched.' It is not I, it is the Lord who says,
' These shall go into everlasting punishment,
and those into everlasting life,' and how the
Lord, with His big heart of love, tender to
everybody, even to the beasts, how the Lord
could combine that with such an awful prospect, is something we have never fathomed to
this hour. If you want to say, ' I do not believe
in everlasting punishment,' remember you are
at perfect liberty to say it. If it is your judgment, then it is yours, but please observe you
can never quote the authority of the Lord
Christ for that. It is awful to think that His
authority is on the other side. You have got to
face up to that. I suppose the two difficulties
men have felt when they have allowed themselves to brood upon this matter are these.
First, we say, we have all said, How could any
one be happy in heaven, how could the saints
of heaven sing their song if they knew that there
were souls—even one soul—suffering in hopeless misery ? To that there is no answer. But
is not it possible that a little light may be drawn
from what we see in this present world ? Are
not there people in Glasgow who are perfectly
happy, thoroughly enjoying themselves, and

all the time within a stone's-throw there are men and women in hopeless misery ? You see it can be done, and if you answer, as I have no doubt the keener among you would answer at once, that these are worldly people, these are not the inhabitants of heaven, my experience is, it is generally worldly people who talk like that. The saints rather bow the head and say, ' Shall not the Judge of all the earth do right ? '

I fancy our other profound difficulty is this. How can God be love ? how can God care and be a Father and wish us well and have the power to give us the best, and yet for ever have creatures in hopeless misery ? Again there is no answer, but again does not this present world suggest that it may be possible ? Is not God love to-day ? is not God infinitely kind to-day ? and yet to-day are there none who have committed the unpardonable sin which can never be forgiven, neither in this life nor the life to come ? May there not be a fixity of heart, a deadness like that of the nether millstone, owing to our free-will working as well as the love of God ? There is not one of us here this morning, there is not one of us, in pew or pulpit, who does not long with all the passion of his heart for universal restoration ; there is not one here who does not crave that ultimately

all should be blessed ; but the Lord has been
our light, the Lord has been the revealer of the
Father, and it is the Lord who says, ' Where
their worm dieth not and the fire is never
quenched.' It is the Lord who says, ' These
shall go away into everlasting punishment.' I
want to speak in the right tone, I don't want to
speak harshly. I am like a man groping in the
dark, but with one hand I grip Christ, and I
say, Brother, would not it be awful to awaken
and find that you were wrong and the Lord
was right ? ' Seek ye the Lord while He may
be found, call ye upon Him while He is near :
let the wicked forsake his way, and the unrighteous man his thoughts : and let him return
to the Lord, and He will have mercy upon
him.'

The next thing which our blessed Saviour tells
us is that He Himself is going to be our judge :
' When the Son of Man shall come in His glory.'
Our judge is not God, the Father ; our judge
is Christ, the Son, and you know that is as
stupendous as it is beautiful. Think how
stupendous it is. Here is Christ, born in a
manger, living for thirty years in a little
cottage, going about among humble people,
doing little deeds of kindness, and then He
says, ' I am going to judge mankind.' It is
either arrogance raised to the point of madness,

or it is truth, and I do not think that any fair review would ever charge the Lord with arrogance. And if it is the truth, your Carpenter of Nazareth is God, and you have got to bow before Him and say, 'My Lord and my God.' All well enough to say, I love the Carpenter of Nazareth ; I like to watch Him talking with the children, watching the sparrows, moving through the harvest ; but mark you, your only source of knowledge of that Carpenter tells you that He said, 'I am going to judge the world.' Then how beautiful it is that you and I are going to be judged by a man, by one who bore our burdens, by one who knew our frame, by one who understands us perfectly. The other day there came into the vestry a man who again had given way to drink. When I asked him what was the cause of it, he answered something like this : 'I was down and out, my business tottering, my home unhappy, and I gave way to drink.' If I had judged him, what would he have said ? He would have said, 'You do not understand ; you had never a business that was tottering ; you were never unhappy at home.' But if I could have said to him, 'Brother, I have been down and out, I have come through all that you have, and yet God brought me through,' my very presence would have judged him. It is so with the Lord. He was tempted in all points like as we are, yet without sin. He was down and out when every disciple forsook Him and fled; and He is going to be our judge. I could imagine some daring soul on the Day of Judgment, if the judge was God the Father, saying, 'Thou who dwellest yonder, far away in the light that never fades, you do not understand.' Nobody ever can say that to Christ; I think just His presence will be the judgment.

One thing more I have got to say, and it is this, that our Lord—apart from the figure altogether—teaches us the principle of the Last Judgment, and the principle is this: it is the discharge or the neglect of the common charities of life. May I say it again? It is the discharge or the neglect of the common humanities of life—visiting the prisoner, cheering the sick, giving bread to the hungry, clothing the naked; and that is but a short and swift summation of what we call the charities of life. Are not you surprised? You thought character was going to be the test in the Last Judgment; you thought the spirit of Christ was going to be the test—'If any man have not the spirit of Christ he is none of His'; you thought your relationship to Christ was going to be the test. You are perfectly right, and yet do you see how

beautifully the Lord puts it? First, is not it
our common actions that are the best test of
character? Is there anything else that shows
character like the common actions of unnumbered days? I think the war taught us
that. You had men in the war who did very
wonderful deeds, some of them got the Victoria
Cross, and we all honour them and God
honours them; there were beautiful great
deeds. Were they tests of character? What
about the Divorce Court? It is not things like
that that tell you what a man is. Did you
never know any one who prayed, yet you could
not trust their word? Did you never know any
one who gave great sums away, yet you found
their motives were impure? But the daily
common charities of life, pursued through
years when there is nobody to notice—our Lord
says you are going to be judged by character,
and that is the test of character. Somebody
said, you remember, that you never ought to
judge a man by a single action, but if you had
to, let it be a common one. Take the spirit of
Christ. Are you going to be judged by whether
or not you have the spirit of Christ? Now
don't talk vaguely. What is the spirit of Christ?
What is it? You know we think of it as such
a great mystery that we miss its meaning.
What is it? I say it is the spirit that brought

Him to the manger, it is the spirit that kept
Him quiet in Nazareth for thirty years, it is
the spirit that made Him move among men,
teaching them, healing them, helping them,
doing them good ; and if that is your life, you
have got the spirit of Christ. You do not know
it ? Of course you don't ; none of the saved
knew it, they were all amazingly surprised when
the Lord told how He reckoned them. And
you may have the spirit of Christ this morning
if you go out and be kindly, charitable, helpful ;
and yet you may never know it till the judgment comes. You say, I am going to be judged
by my relationship to Christ. Yes, you are.
When the Lord was here, with whom, tell me,
did He identify Himself ? Was it with Herod ?
' Go tell that fox.' Was it with the Pharisees ?
' Woe unto you, Pharisees.' The Lord identified Himself with the poor, with the needy,
with the last, with the least, with the lost ; and
He is the same yesterday and to-day and for
ever. And if the Lord is identified with all who
are in need, then every time you help a man
in need you are brought into relationship with
Christ.

It has been very difficult—not difficult to
speak the truth, but to speak the truth in the
right spirit this morning. I trust I have done
it tenderly, and I simply want to ask you to

remember that all of us have got to appear before the judgment seat of Christ, and therefore should not we all revise our lives this morning, lest at the end, when far off there is music, for us it should be wailing and gnashing of teeth ?

VIII

'And they compel one Simon a Cyrenian, who passed by, coming out of the country, the father of Alexander and Rufus, to bear His cross.'—Mark xv. 21.

I WANT you, please, to note the words that are employed in verses 20 and 22. In this, the greatest hour of history, every word is of supreme significance ; thus we read in the 20th verse, ' They led Him out to crucify Him.' And then we read in the 22nd verse, ' They bring Him unto Golgotha.' These two words are just a little window on to the supreme physical exhaustion of the Saviour in this the greatest hour of His agony. You see, when He left the Praetorium they were leading Him ; when they came to Golgotha they were bearing Him. He had started walking ; He had stumbled ; He had needed the support of these strong hands, and I think nothing could more eloquently speak to us of the full true humanity of Christ than just the awful physical weakness of that hour. You see, for fifteen hours, since the hour of the Last Supper, our Lord had suffered the most awful strain, strain of body, agony of mind. ' My soul is sorrowful, even unto death.' Now, He was so utterly forspent that He staggered and stumbled in the way. 'He was a man of sorrows and acquainted with grief.' All this, my brother, He bore for you and me when He might have had hosts of angels at His bidding. Here, as at the outset of His mission, He refused to turn stones into bread, refused to avail Himself of anything that might break the bond between Him and us when He was dying in our room and stead.

Well now, it was the custom of these Roman soldiers to make the criminal carry his own cross, but in this instance that was quite impossible, and the question was, what were they to do? No Roman would have touched the horrid thing—Roman shoulders were not meant for that. To have made a home-born Jew bear it would have been to court uproar; and just then, coming down the way that probably led from the uplands about Bethany, they saw the very person that they wanted. Others were travelling in companies, this man was travelling alone. His dark skin showed that he was a foreigner; his costume showed he was an African; he was a stranger who had no kith or kin, he was far from home, probably friendless. This was the very person that they wanted. I don't suppose these soldiers pitied Christ; half an hour before they had been mocking Him; they were irritated at the loss of time, things were not going according to their programme, and they cried, ' You, you blackamore, come here ! ' (You know he was known afterwards as Simeon Niger.) And him they compelled to bear the cross. This Gospel is very rich in vivid touches ; is there a touch so vivid as this one ?—the sinking Saviour, the irritated soldiers, the dark-skinned foreigner coming from the country, and over everything the blue heaven, and the birds singing as they used to sing when Jesus was a happy boy at home.

I want this morning for a little while just to try and show you some of the teaching of that story, and in the first place, will you notice how a man can serve Christ though he is utterly ignorant who He is. I don't imagine for a single moment that Simon had ever seen the Lord before. Possibly, and indeed probably, he had never even heard His name, for the Lord's name had not penetrated Africa, and it was in Africa Simon had his home. Probably he had just arrived the other day. Then, you observe, he was coming from the country ; that means he had his lodging in the country. At Passover the city was so full that many had to get lodgings in the country, and therefore that morning, coming to the city, he had no idea who the prisoner was—he was doing something for somebody he did not know. The strange thing is that he was called to serve somebody whom he had never heard of; called to help in a great hour which was going to change the future of the world; called not to a little service, but to a great service, so splendid and unique that any of Jesus' disciples might have envied him. Mary broke the spikenard on His head, Martha made Him a supper in the evening, Joseph served by giving Him a grave, Lazarus by giving Him a cottage, but all these services, however beautiful, are not to be matched with this of Simon when he relieved the Lord of the burden of His cross. To him and to him alone was it given to help our Saviour in His deepest need, to him to relieve Him of His cross when all the others forsook Him and fled. And how profoundly significant it is that this service, such a glorious service, was rendered to the Christ he did not know. And then one thinks of the parable of Jesus about the Last Judgment of the world: 'Come, ye blessed of My Father, inherit the kingdom that is prepared for you; for I was hungry and ye gave Me meat: I was thirsty, and ye gave Me drink,' and then the blessed are going to say in frank astonishment, 'Lord, when saw we Thee an hungred, or thirsty?' You see, evidently in the mind of Christ thousands are serving Him who never knew Him—in little actions, in the kindly loving deeds, in the little offices of courtesy and love ; and what is to hinder us widening out that thought to the great services of men written in the history of the world ? The men who built these highways across continents—they were serving Christ although they never knew it ; the men who constructed railways across Africa—they were serving Christ although they never knew it ; the man who invented printing, though he may never have thought about the Lord, he too has been a magnificent evangelist. So was it with Simon ; he knew nothing of the prisoner, he had not the least idea whom he served when he carried the cross up the hill, but he was serving the Lord Christ, he was helping on the coming of His kingdom. He has got his reward.

And then, another thought embodied in our story is just the unexpectedness of life. This was the great hour in Simon's history, and it just came to him like a bolt out of the blue. You have got to picture him that beautiful spring morning leaving the cottage where he had had his bed, crossing the fields brilliant with anemones, going up the pathway to the city, meditating on the goodness of the Lord in bringing him to the city of his dreams and allowing him to see the holy place. He had

come there to celebrate the Passover, and that
done, he was going home again to his wife and
his two boys in Africa who had been praying
for him every day ; and just then, dreaming
his own dreams and meditating upon the God
of Jacob, he was gripped and brought into the
presence of the Lord.   And one feels how it
would come to him all in a moment that he
was present at the greatest hour of history, the
hour for which the world had been waiting,
the hour that the Psalmist had foreseen, the
hour that the prophets had foretold, and it just
came to him without any sound of trumpets.
Simon dreaming his own dreams, his greatest
hour met him by the way.   And I scarcely
need to tell you how true that is of life.   Have
not we a proverb in almost every language
that it is the unexpected thing that happens?
Joseph came out to see how his brothers fare,
and Joseph is never going to see his home again.
David in the morning is king, and when night
falls he is flying from his son.   Matthew is
sitting at the receipt of custom ; somebody
speaks to him and calls him, and the future is
never to be the same again.   How often our
sorrows take us unexpectedly ! How often our
joys take us unexpectedly ! How often the
things we have looked for never come, the
things that we never looked for have arrived :

all of which should teach us not that life is chance, but that our highest wisdom is to trust Him when we know not what an hour may bring forth.   How often Jesus meets us unexpectedly when our thoughts are busy upon something else ! And I beg of you never to forget that that is how the Lord is going to come, in an hour when you never think of it. If you and I were in the hands of fate, life's unexpectedness would be its tragedy ; but we are not, thank God, in the hands of fate.   We are in the hands of One who loves us and who knows us ;   One who sees the fall of every sparrow, in whose eternal love is no to-morrow, whose everlasting purposes embrace, as Wordsworth says :

  ' Whose everlasting purposes embrace all accidents, converting them to good.'

' Almost by the merest chance I met the Lord.' I dare say Simon spoke like that.   ' Had I overslept myself by half an hour I never would have stumbled on the Saviour.'   My dear hearer, he did not oversleep himself, because the Lord God is merciful and gracious and loved him from the foundation of the world.

Then the last lesson which I want to touch on is this, how men are blessed by the things they are compelled to.   As the years went by and Simon's hair grew white, I am perfectly certain he often thought of that. Will you please observe he was compelled, his wishes were not consulted in the matter. Very probably he was rebellious ; this was degrading to an honest Jew, and then, was not he due in the Temple at that hour, and was not this interfering with his plans ? But it was no use struggling ; he was one, the might of Imperial Rome legion ; better to yield to the inevitable, although he did it with a curse within his heart. And the beautiful thing is that just that bitter task to which he was compelled proved the glory of his life. There is no question that he became a Christian. Alexander and Rufus were members of the Church. Mark talks as if everybody knew them ; they were familiar figures in the Church at Rome, and all the blessing and the altered home, and the new deepened spiritual relationships came from something to which he was compelled. If he had had his way that morning, if nobody had interfered with him, if he had been allowed to do just as he pleased, he would have gone back to Africa, and we would never have heard of him. But the bitter thing he had to do, doing it perhaps with a curse within his heart, was just what proved his blessing. There are things in your life you are compelled to do ; there are things in your life you are compelled to bear. Sometimes you think that if you were only free from them life would become sunshine and music, but one of the deepest lessons of this life is that things we are compelled to are the road to character and heaven. Accept that task you have got to do, accept that burden you are compelled to bear. The wonderful thing is how often it proves the very cross of Christ; it brings you into His fellowship, it deepens your character, it steadies you, it gives you the kingdom and the patience of the Lord, it draws you into sympathy with others. Simon became quite a noble character through the bitter thing he was compelled to. Has not it been the same with you and me?

IX

THESE beautiful poppies that decorate our tablet, and this wreath of evergreens that hangs before you, suggest two thoughts that rise into our minds and inevitably mix and mingle there. In the first place, this is Remembrance Sunday, and you and I are remembering the fallen, some of them very dear to us, who used to sit and worship with us in the sanctuary here, and on that great duty of remembrance, and how Christ has turned our sorrow into joy, I hope to talk for a little while this morning. But then, arising in our minds there is another thought, and of course that is the thought of peace. We remember how the boys died hoping that this war was going to end war. I am quite sure that in all our hearts this morning there is a very deep and strong desire that we should have peace among the nations. Dr. Jowett, whose name is in all our churches, was recently at the Congress in Copenhagen. When he came home one of our newspapers got him to record his impression, and he told us how his deepest impression gathered from the Conference was that the world was hungering for universal peace. He had talked with thoughtful men from Germany, he had talked with thoughtful men from France, he had talked with thoughtful men from Greece, he had talked with thoughtful men from far Japan. Behind all governments, behind all politicians, all diplomatists, all militarists, he said, everywhere the dumb heart of the race was hungering after peace. Don't you think that is true? If I were to ask you this morning, as has been done in some of our English churches, if I were to ask all of you who have the determination there shall be no more war, to rise up to your feet, there is not a soul here that would continue sitting. It is one of the most recent charges made against the Church (of course the Church is quite familiar with charges) that her will to peace is not nearly so evident as was her will to war. The Church threw herself into that great war, as I am proud to say she did, but that was far more evident than the expressed desire to-day that we ought to have peace among the nations. I trust we shall always listen quietly to the charges of those who are without. While you can learn a great deal from your friends, you can generally learn more from your enemies. But I venture to say that that charge is just as ignorant as it is malicious. In fact, it reminds me of something that happened long ago. I remember in Thurso a lady, an ardent temperance reformer, coming to my revered senior colleague—his name was Dr. Ross Taylor ; he was ordained in '29 by the hands of Edward Irving ; what an old story does it seem to-day—and she said to him (this ardent temperance worker), ' Sir, I have listened to you for so many years, and I have never heard you mention temperance.' He said, with the bow of antique courtesy, ' Madam, I preach two temperance sermons every Sunday.' What he meant was, and it was perfectly correct, that whenever you preach Christ you are preaching temperance. And what I mean is, and I am perfectly correct, than whenever you preach Christ you are preaching peace—' Glory to God in the highest, on earth peace, to men goodwill.' We crown Him as the Prince of Peace. Whenever you declare the evangel, you are talking about peace—that of God, the peace the world can never give and never take away. Whenever you preach Christ you are talking about peace of conscience, through the peace-speaking blood of the Lord. But don't forget that whenever you preach Christ, you preach One in whom is neither Jew nor Greek, Barbarian or Scythian, bond or free. You preach the brotherhood of man.

Well now, that is why I have chosen this text this morning ; because it unites the Spirit of the Lord with the thought of peace that is in every heart this morning, and I want you to try and follow me while I discuss it.

You see, Paul is talking to these Corinthian Christians, and that Church at Corinth was remarkable in this, remarkable for its variety of gifts. I do not suppose there was a man in Corinth, I scarcely suppose there was a woman, who did not possess some spiritual gift. One man had the gift of healing ; another had the gift of miracles ; a third the gift of prophecy or of preaching (for of course New Testament prophecy is not prediction) ; and a fourth had the gift of tongues. I suppose in all the churches that Paul founded there was not a single one that had such a variety of gifts as had the Church at Corinth. Had they only felt that they were one, had they only felt they were members of a body, had the eye never said to the ear 'I have no need of thee,' or the foot to the hand 'I have no need of thee,' what a wonderful Church it would have been. But instead of that they were jealous, they were covetous, there was strife, there was party division, there was war. Paul's heart was

almost breaking. How it weighed down that
gallant soul, how it led him to his knees. How
they had treated God in that darkened little
world of Corinth it is almost impossible to say.
Then he comes, led by the Holy Ghost, and he
says, ' Brothers, there is only one way if you
are ever going to have peace.' Like a bird
singing at heaven's gate, he sings it in the
thirteenth chapter. Covet, if you must covet,
but don't covet the showy gifts ; covet the best
ones. Did you ever notice when we covet what
another has it is not generally the best in him
we covet ? Paul says, if you must covet, covet
the best gifts, but for you there is only one way,
that is the way of love. Do you know it was an
extraordinarily bold thing for Paul to write to
Corinth a chapter about love, for Corinth was
the most sensual city in the world, and to every
Corinthian love was just immoral ? (I could
not exaggerate the state of things at Corinth.)
And then Paul comes and he says, ' Children,
I am not talking about love like that (he has got
to coin a new word to express it), it is goodwill, it is brotherhood, it is co-operation, it is
something that thinks no evil, never vaunts
itself, is not puffed up, that beareth all things,
that believeth all things, that hopeth all things.'
Well now, don't you see, that great argument which applied to Corinth applies equally

to the nations of the world, and applies to them just for this reason, that every nation has its peculiar gift. You may differ about nationality, you may think of it in various ways, but every historian will admit that every nation has its peculiar gift—even Mr. Buckle, who is not ready to admit anything, most willingly admits that. By the law, of course, of their national history, by the influence of soil and climate, by their peculiar struggle for existence, by the kind of scenes that they look upon, every nation, in the ordering of God, has its peculiar gift. The Hebrew people had their gift : it was an awful sense of God. The Greek people had their gift, an exquisite appreciation of the beautiful. The Roman people had their gift, the splendid gift of law and order, the power for colonising the great world. Would it be wrong to say the Russians have the gift of tongues ? Did you ever hear more extraordinary linguists ? Has not Scotland had the gift of prophecy ? Has not Britain got the gift of governing ? Nobody can govern like Britain. Has not France the appreciation of the beautiful ? Oh, if they could only have realised that they are all members of one body, that the foot cannot say to the hand 'I have no need of thee,' that the eye cannot say to the ear 'I have no need of thee,' what a glorious world it would have been.

I venture to say there would not be one man in
Anderston or Cranstonhill unemployed. But
instead of that you have strikes, you have got
nation rising against nation, you have got the
horrid tragedy of the Great War. Paul just
comes to us, or if you like it, the Spirit of God
comes to us, and He says, ' If you want to
covet, covet, but always covet the best gifts.'
Don't covet the lands of Germany, don't covet
the colonies of Germany ; covet the thought
and poetry of Goethe. But with all your covet-
ing there is only one way, and it is the way of
loving, willing co-operation, it is love, as Paul
sings it in the thirteenth chapter. Of course,
when any one says that, you feel that the man
talking is a sentimental dreamer. You are out
for practical politics, and this is not practical
politics. If Paul, instead of being a theologian,
had only been a statesman, he never would
have suggested this solution. Paul was one of
the greatest statesmen who ever lived. I will
venture to say that in all that Roman Empire
there was not a statesman so able as Paul. He
had a massive and majestic intellect, he had a
disengaged heart ; he never strove for party, he
had a vision that was imperial of the world.
Paul spent his life travelling up and down
seeing the problems at first hand, moving from
country into country, and then from city into

city, and yet Paul—statesman, man of sober intellect—gets up and says, ' Brother, there is only one way, and that is the way of love.' Not diplomacy, though it may do a little— diplomacy breaks down just when you need it. Not statesmanship, so-called—statesmanship did not avert the war. Paul says it is love, and he believes it. You see, this great soul believed that Christ must reign till He had put all enemies under His feet. He was convinced that the kingdom of this world was going to become the kingdom of his Lord. This song of music, like many another song, was going to prove more powerful than dynamite, not because Paul was a great genius, but because Christ was the dynamo ; He was the Power of God. The question is, do we believe it ? We call our statesmen practical men, and the preacher a dreamer. It is the dreamers that triumph in the end. The singular thing is that the whole course of history has been tending to prove that Paul is right. Everything that you call progress, and I suppose you believe in progress, at the very heart of it has had the displacing of brute force and the bringing in of love. There are people who disbelieve in progress, who don't hold that the world is getting better (they put it that it need not necessarily get better, but what they mean is that it is not), people who have not the slightest hope that this idealism is going to conquer, and these people are what you call ' opportunists.' What I want you to note is this, that in many a lesser circle this is exactly what has happened, and if it has triumphed in the lesser circles, why should it not triumph in the great one of humanity ?

Suppose I pursue that argument for a moment. Think of the circle of the home. You know once at home love was subordinate. When the family emerges on to the page of history it is not love, it is force, that is supreme. A man then, when he wanted to win a wife, did not win her by the ways of love, but went out and killed somebody and brought home the scalp upon his belt. Or in other countries, in those far days when a man desired to win a wife, he did not woo her in a loving way ; he captured the woman in a raid. Similarly, the right of the father over his child : it began by being unlimited by love—witness the story of Abraham, who could slaughter Isaac. And even in ancient Rome the father's power included the right of murdering his child. (Thank God it very rarely happened, because the heart is bigger than your law.) There it was, written in the laws of early Rome, that a father, if he wanted, could kill his child. And

the point is, don't you see, that even down to
history it was not love that was supreme at
home, it was brute force. And then came the
Lord Jesus Christ breathing His spirit on the
home, taking the force that always must be
there and clothing it with love. You and I,
born and bred in Scotland, and who have had
the inestimable blessing of a Christian home,
tell me, has not it been a magnificent success ?
There in the little circle of the home there was
only one way, and there it has triumphed.
Why should not it triumph in the great circle
of the world ?

Or again, take another lesser circle ; take
the sphere of school. There was a time, not so
long ago, when school was ruled by force.
Somebody has said that an unwhipped child
was regarded as a missed opportunity. My
father often used to tell us of his experience in
schooldays. He went to a little parish school
in one of the most beautiful districts in beautiful
Morayshire. The dominie, a disappointed man,
was awful and terrible in his chastisements.
He never dreamed of love ; his one argument,
the cane. Then came great souls like Dr.
Arnold : Dr. Arnold on fire for his Master,
and he loved the boys with his whole heart,
and he honoured them, he trusted them ; and
now to-day into all our schools has spread the

spirit of love, goodwill, co-operation ; and who is going to tell me that it has not been a magnificent success ? Why, a hundred years ago nobody ever could have dreamed of a little girl going willingly to school. Shakespeare, who knew things, does not he talk of the schoolboy ' creeping like snail unwillingly to school ' ? But I know little girls in Glasgow, and every morning they are eager even to leave the mother to go to school. You see, in the limited circle of the school, a place of most intricate relationships, where you have got youth and age always touching one another, Paul's way has been tried, and it has proved the most magnificent success.

I shall just mention one other sphere, and it is the sphere of the mission-field. And in order that I may make it evident to you, suppose you and I think of Livingstonia. I wonder if you ever read the book of Dr. Elmslie's (it is a little out of date nowadays) called *Among the Wild Ngoni* ? Well now, I should like some of you to read it, and there you read that before Christ came—and Dr. Elmslie is a shrewd son of Caithness and never the man who would venture to exaggerate—the ruling powers were force and fear and fraud. Love—it was never dreamed of. And the result was, life was just a hell for the women and also for the men.

There was no security ; it was a life of terror.
And then Christ came where force and fear
and fraud ruled, and I don't think it is too much
to say that to-day love, not sentiment, is the
ruling power in Livingstonia. Is there anybody here who ever visited it ? If you have,
stand up and tell us that it has been a magnificent success.

Don't you see, in the circle of the home love
has been tried, and triumphed. In the circle
of the school love has been tried, and triumphed.
In great regions like beautiful Livingstonia love
has been tried, and triumphed. And yet, you
have men who will rise up and say to the whole
world, It is just a dream ; don't try it, it is no
use. Surely it is. Will you support the League
of Nations ? You know it wants our national
support. Will you make evident your will for
peace, just as you did your will for war ? But,
above everything, will you ask, will you pray,
will you will, for the coming of His kingdom,
which is love ? Then, and then only, we will
have the brotherhood of nations, and the awful-
ness of war will have vanished quite away.

X

'But sanctify the Lord God in your hearts: and be ready always to give an answer to every man that asketh your reason for the hope that is in you.'—1 Peter iii. 15.

A MINISTER, in the ordinary course of his ministry, has got to present his gospel in very different ways. He has always got to remember he is not preaching in a vacuum, but preaching to men and women for their peculiar trials and troubles and intellectual difficulties. I therefore make no apology for turning aside a little this morning from the direct message of the Gospel, just to endeavour to give you a reason for the faith that is in you in regard to God. I want you to observe how the Apostle says ' Sanctify the Lord God in your hearts,' and then immediately goes on to say, You ought to have a reason for that faith. And I should like this morning to conduct a line of thought that will require your very close attention, but which, if grasped, I think is a reason of extraordinary power for our faith in the God of Scripture.

The point is this. In our Bible, as you are all aware, you have one definite and particular view of God. It is quite unlike the view of any

other sacred book; it is peculiar to the Bible.
The interesting thing is that it never changes;
in all its large essentials it is just the same, from
the Book of Genesis right on to the Book of
Revelation. There is not one God of the Old
Testament and another God of the New. Our
Lord did not turn His back upon the Old when
He called God His Father. Our Lord said, the
Father is the God of Abraham, of Isaac, and of
Jacob. Of course the apprehension of that God
is a thing that is constantly changing. God is
far too great to understand all at once. A
great deal of the glory of the Bible is just how
steadily, from first to last, you see the soul of
man coming to a deeper apprehension of the
unchanging God. You look at Ben Lomond
from the east, and then you look at Ben
Lomond from the west; then you look at it on
a day like yesterday, then you look at it in the
mists of November; and it is always different,
but it is always Ben Lomond—you never dream
of saying 'That is Ben Nevis.' And it is like that
with the God of Scripture. The point is, that
when the Bible was written our modern knowledge did not exist. All that we now mean by
science, in the days of the Bible was not to be
found. It would not be too much to say that
from that day to this heaven and earth have
passed away. The world was then the centre;

it is now a little insignificant planet on the out-skirts. And I think the first thing any one would say is this, that the God you find in an old book like the Bible can never be the God that is required and postulated by our modern knowledge. And if I can show you, however imperfectly, that, granted there is a God at all (because anything else is quite outwith our argument), the God demanded by our modern knowledge is the very God you discover in the Scripture, written before that knowledge was ever thought of, would not it be a powerful argument that what you have got there is a revelation, something inspired in the hearts of men by God Himself? I want to conduct that argument this morning. It is a little apart from the usual Gospel preaching, but I am here to help to build you up in your most holy faith.

Well now, first, modern knowledge tells us that if there be a God, He must be one. The thought of two, twenty, or ten thousand gods has been put to flight by all we have come to learn. I am perfectly well aware that in the Great War men were tempted to turn back to that; men were tempted to say, God cannot be omnipotent; there must be another god fighting against Him (just as John Stuart Mill said that God had matter fighting against Him), if you want to explain the war. One of

our great novelists, who knows much more of
life than of theology, popularised that view.
That, of course, is just an imaginative way of
escaping from a real difficulty, and it has got
no basis in our knowledge whatever. Suppose
you found, for instance, certain laws working
in your garden, and when you travelled to the
stars you find that totally other laws are working there. Well, of course, you would conclude
that different hands had been making this great
universe. But all knowledge has been teaching
us that the very opposite is the case. The law
that regulates the falling of the apple is regu-
lating the planets up in heaven. The law that
moulds the little tiny weed moulded the giant
pine out in California. The law that shapes the
most minute crystal is the very law that shapes
the elements of suns. As I have put it more
than once, we do not live in a multiverse, you
and I live in a universe. And all our modern
knowledge comes along and says, I am not saying I believe in God, but am saying that if
there be a God, that God must be one. And
the extraordinary thing is this, that that is the
God you find in the Bible page. The Bible was
written thousands of years ago, before men
knew anything about science at all. Mark you,
if you found it in other sacred books as well,
your argument would go, but you don't. The

only other one you find it in is the Koran of
Mohammed, and the Koran admittedly takes
all its truth from the Old Testament, and all its
theology from the Old Testament. You turn
to the sacred books of Persia—two gods, one of
light, one of darkness. You turn to the sacred
books of India—gods innumerable (still so in
Hinduism). In Greece there was a god for
every element—one for the fire, one for the
air, one for the sea. And the Romans were so
tolerant of gods that if they conquered a country
they took its gods and put them in the Pantheon
along with their own. And over against all
that, back in these dim ages when the unity of
nature never had been dreamed of, you have
got the unity of God in Scripture. Well now,
can you explain it ? Do you really think, as a
reasonable man, it was excogitated by the
human brain ? To me, I confess, it is just
irresistible argument for the revelation in the
Holy Scripture.

Well now, I go a little further. Modern
knowledge tells us that if there be a God—*if*
there be a God (we make the assumption),
that God must be rational ; that is to say,
intelligent, with an intelligence akin to mine,
although it may be infinitely greater. I would
fain make you understand how philosophy has
come to that. It is not just a matter of detail—

'Flower in the crannied wall'—the man of
science will tell you he can explain the flower
in the crannied wall without the hypothesis of
God. You remember when a great French
astronomer came with his book of astronomy
to Napoleon, and Napoleon reading it said,
'Sir, it is a wonderful book, but there is nothing
of God in it,' the astronomer answered, 'Sire,
I have no need of that hypothesis.' Hundreds
of scientific men to-day will explain about the
sheen that is on the wing of the bird, the marks
upon the back of the tiger, the fins upon the
fish, the convolutions in the eye, without the
hypothesis of God. You see you cannot reach
it that way. The way that philosophy reaches
it is like this. Suppose I give you a book, and
suppose I ask you to read it. Well now, you
look at it, and there are words and letters, it is
written in the English tongue, but you cannot
make anything of that book ; you don't know
what it is talking about ; you turn it upside
down, it is all chaos. You at once conclude,
either it is written by a madman or the letters
have been tossed together by the wind. But,
on the other hand, if you understand the book,
though perhaps there are passages in it far
beyond you, and you cannot get them yet, still
if you understand it, don't you see the conclusion irresistible, that that book was written

by a mind kindred to your own—infinitely greater, possibly—the mind of a Shakespeare or a Milton, but at any rate a mind kindred to your own ?   The same thing with music.   I give Mr. Turner[1] a piece of music.   There are the notes, there are the bars and all the rest of it ; and I ask him to read it and play it. He tries to play it, and he says, ' This is nonsense ; other beings may understand it, I cannot ; it has no kinship with my mind, there is no melody lurking there.'   But if he understands it, if he sits down and plays it, although now and again he comes on a passage that he says is very difficult, don't you see it was written by a mind kindred to his own, perhaps greater ?   Don't you and I talk of the ' book ' of nature ? and the strange thing about the book of nature is, that you can understand it.   Don't you see, if you could not there would be no science, because science is just ordered knowledge.   You think of Sir Isaac Newton sitting down before the book of nature.   He understands it, though sometimes he bows his head and says, ' It is too difficult for me ' ; but he gets his great laws out of it.   Don't you see, philosophy says—not from the roadside, but from the whole scheme of things—*if* there be a God, if I grant you *that*, and I *will* do it for

[1] Organist of Wellington Church.

a moment, if there be a God, that God is rational, intelligent, because I understand the things He writes.

Once again, you know it is a marvellous thing that before there was ever any philosophy of that kind at all, there in the Bible you have got a God who says, ' Come and let us reason together.' Not a blind power that makes you do what he wants—a power that gives you liberty, a power that pleads with you, argues with you, treats you as a reasonable being. And once more I want to know, do you think man excogitated that ? Is that what you get in the sacred book of India ? Is that what you get in the Persian *Avesta* ? Is not it far more likely they have been revealed ?

Once again (I trust I make this plain to you), modern thought comes to us and says to us, Suppose I grant you there is a God ; I am perfectly convinced He must be moral. You know that is perhaps the most glorious thought the great philosopher Kant ever lodged in the human brain. If he had done nothing else, he has ennobled all humanity by working out that thought and getting it lodged in the human brain. I wonder if I could tell you what Kant meant by the moral end of nature creation. Kant said, in every man there is a conscience— it may be dim, rudimentary, seared with a hot iron, disregarded ; never mind, in every man there is a conscience, something that says to him ' Thou shalt ' and ' Thou shalt not,' and to Kant it was the most wonderful thing in the whole universe, except the shining of the stars. Well now, Kant's argument was this : Kant said—and it is a masterly and significant argument—Suppose that in the world without I find nothing to answer to that conscience in man ; suppose the world goes on independent of whether a man disregards or obeys his conscience, then nobody can ever prove to me that this is a world built by a moral Creator. But, Kant says, if in the long-run the world is on the side of the man who does his duty ; if, in the long-run, if a man disregards his conscience the world rises up to shatter and crush him, Kant says, then there *is* a moral Creator. In the long-run, mark you—the philosopher takes large views.

Kant could have illustrated it, for instance, from the drunkard. You take the case of a man who is a drunkard. Well now, a drunkard knows perfectly—he may brazen it out, he may seem very happy, but a drunkard knows perfectly that he is doing what is wrong. Independent of the consequences, there is something in his breast that makes him say, ' Thou shalt not be a drunkard.' Well now, Kant would say, Supposing a man could be a drunkard and nothing happened, the world just go on to him as it used to do when he was a temperate, sober young man, Kant would say, I never can prove that the Creator was a moral power, the world has not been built along the lines of conscience. Kant would say, What is the truth? The man becomes a drunkard; the little bit of matter he calls his feet, he cannot use them; the little bit of matter he calls his eyes, he cannot see out of them, he sees double; his hand ought to be steady, look how it shakes; he loses his power of gripping things. Then you take his business relations. Where is his business? It is all gone; he is almost a beggar. You take his wife and children—does he love them? Sometimes you would think he hates them; wants to make his son a drunkard. The whole universe is up against that man, smashing him, crushing him into nothing. In other words, the power that made the world is the power that makes the conscience. If you have been disregarding your conscience, the world is up against you, and sooner or later gets the better of you. Of course, Kant said, you are not to confuse this with the bad man being prosperous—the prosperous man may be the shallowest, poorest, most dried-up creature in the world. Now, is it not an extraordinary thing that that view of our modern philosophy is what you get in the Bible ? You do not get it in the books of India, of Greece. The Greek gods did not care a snap for morality so long as you performed the ritual. Savage gods never care for conduct ; all you have got to do is certain prescribed things, and you get off. But here, in a book that dates from the dim dawn, God loves righteousness, God hates evil. Let a man obey, and he is like the green bay tree ; let him disobey, and he is like the chaff which the wind drives to and fro. ' God is of purer eyes than to behold iniquity.' Where does that come from ? How did that thought get lodged in Jewish minds when neither in Persian nor in Indian minds, equally spiritual, equally subtle, did it ever get a place ? Well, I do think the most reasonable explanation is just this, that our Bible is an inspired book, and that that has been revealed by God Himself.

I have only one thing more I want to say to complete this argument, and it is this. Your modern man of science says to you, Now, suppose I grant for a moment that there be a God, well I am bound to admit that He is a God to whom man must be infinitely dear. You see, for a moment you have got to take the standpoint of the evolutionist. I don't care whether you are one or not—some of us could not think without evolution as a category. You have got to take that standpoint for a moment, and what does it mean? It just means that from the dark abysm of time, out of some fiery mists, things have been pressing forward, silently, slowly, through millions of years, from the mollusc and the fish and the reptile and the mammal, till at last it all comes to man—never going any further—nobody ever dreams that there is going to be a creature higher than man. It switches off on to moral and spiritual lines whenever it comes to man. If you grant that there is a God—it is the only assumption I want—just think of it. From millions and millions of years ago He has been toiling, without any break, through all kinds of creatures, until at last the creature He had in His mind from the beginning is made, and He looks at him and calls him Man. Why, if you did a bit of work through five or ten years, it would be very precious to you if you got it right, and God has been doing that bit of work through millions and millions of years, and at last there it is— Adam and Eve. And the man of science says, Yes, if I grant you God, He must be a God to whom man is infinitely dear. Then I come to the old Bible, written before anybody dreamed of evolution, and I read, ' God so loved the world, that He gave His only begotten Son, that whosoever believeth in Him should not perish, but have eternal life.' Don't you see? Your modern knowledge says to you, God must be one—there it is. Your modern philosophy says, God must be rational—'Come, let us reason together.' There it is. Your modern knowledge says, God must be moral—'I the Lord love righteousness, and hate evil.' Your modern knowledge says, If I grant you God, He must think a deal of man ; and the Bible, written long ago by children, says, 'God so loved the world, that whosoever believeth in Him should not perish.'

XI

'If we say we have not sinned, we make Him a liar.'—1 John i. 10.

THIS text is just a little difficult to understand, and the difficulty is of a peculiar kind, because it is not quite so easy to see what is the connection between the conclusion and the premises. 'If we say that we have not sinned,' that is premise ; and 'we make God a liar,' that is the conclusion. There are some texts in Scripture a little difficult to understand because the phraseology is difficult ; and there are some texts hard to understand because they seem to contradict our highest moral sense ; but this is one of those numerous texts where it is a little hard to see the connection between the conclusion and the premises. If John had said, for instance, 'If we say we have not sinned, we are fools,' 'If we say we have not sinned, we know nothing whatever about ourselves,' you would have understood that at once. But John says, 'If we say we have not sinned, we make God—not ourselves—a liar,' and to the thoughtful mind there is just a little difficulty in gathering the connection. Well, I should like to try and make that plain to you, for a minister's greatest task is just the exposition of Scripture, and I want to do it not as a matter of intellectual delight, although to me there are few intellectual delights like sounding the depths of Scripture, but just that I may get home to you careless, comfortable people, perhaps get some of you to go home saying, ' God be merciful to me, a sinner.'

Before we face that question there is one other question I have got to ask and answer, and that is, How is it that people say, ' We have not sinned ' ? It is not just saying it with your lips ; but I want to ask in what peculiar ways do common people like you and me say in their hearts, ' We have not sinned ' ? Well, of course, everybody does it in the first place who conceives that he is perfect, but that is such an extraordinary state of mind and so uncommonly rare that I do not imagine I need touch on it except for a moment. In the course of my long pastoral experience, meeting with all types of men and women, I do not remember a single sane person who ever thought he was perfect. I remember one poor man, but then he was insane, and he also thought that he was Christ. Remember, perfection is your ideal and mine—' Be ye perfect as your Father in heaven is perfect ' ; and I have never put any limits to what the Spirit of God can do for any

man who constantly yields himself up to it.   I
have never put any limits, no matter what a
man's past is, no matter how hard his heart is,
no matter what his circumstances are, to what
the Spirit of God can do for anybody who
opens his heart to Him every morning ; but
at the same time this is the universal Christian
experience.   The more you yield yourself, the
more you hitch your wagon to that star, the
more you wrestle on toward heaven 'gainst
storm and wind and tide—the more you feel
and know you are a sinner.   Paul began by
saying about himself that he was less than the
least of saints.   When he got to know Christ a
great deal better he called himself 'the chief of
sinners.'   Therefore I do not think one need
say anything about that ; there is nobody here
this morning who for one moment conceives
that he is perfect.   If there is, may God have
mercy, not upon your soul, may God have
mercy on your mind.   But then a far com-
moner way than that is for people to deny that
what they have done is sin ; that is to say, to
make excuses for yourself that you would never
dream of making for anybody else.   Of course,
I am not talking about you, I am talking about
myself as well, for there is no man or woman,
no matter how God's grace has gripped them,
who is not always prone to make excuses for his

own conduct that he would never dream of making for anybody else.

For instance, sometimes you read of a man stealing money. Well now, if his neighbour did it, of course he would be a thief, but the man is so earnest he is going to pay, but he wanted time, that in him it is not sin ; or perhaps he gets such a starvation wage that he says he is just taking what he has got a right to, and then he says, ' I have not sinned.' Many of you are tempted to tell lies just because the truth would cause such pain or discomfort to somebody you love, and you say you have not sinned because you have done it out of human kindness. You would never admit that in anybody else. Of course to-day, when people on every hand are breaking the Seventh Commandment, dashing in pieces the covenant of honour and purity, of course they all say that it is love ; love is such a beautiful thing it justifies anything, does it not ? Or perhaps they say it is necessity, and necessity knows no law. In a thousand ways like that to-day people are juggling with their conscience, and just saying, Whatever be the case with others, of course I have not sinned. Perhaps equally common among people who are led by the cold light of intellect rather than by the flaming light of passion, is the thought that sin does not exist ; it is only a dream of fusty theologians, there is no such thing. What is sin ? Now sin, if it is anything, of course, is a transgression of the law of God ; sin is the free act of a free man. Sin is something for which you—nobody else—are responsible ; therefore if we are liable, the punishment, that is the guilt, is a reality, and always with guilt there comes fear. Now when anybody takes up a view of life that just denies the reality of these things, robs them of what is essential in their meaning, don't you see he says, 'We have not sinned' ? If sin is a necessity, a necessary negative if you have got to get a positive, if sin is only imperfection, not a fall down but a fall up, letting the ape and tiger die, only a necessary stage in evolution, if everything is determined by heredity, well, of course, you say you have not sinned ; whatever you have done, that does not exist. These things seem very modern, but they were all present, mark you, with John at Ephesus, and John says, ' If any man says he has not sinned, he makes God a liar.' Now don't you see what it means ? You know if I called a man a liar, what I imply is that that man has been speaking, and probably speaking to me, and when you call God a liar you imply that God has been speaking to you. And John's point is, that whenever and in whatsoever way God speaks, the basis of His speech is the fact of sin. In every voice God uses He talks on the understanding, implied or asserted, that sin is a reality, and therefore, don't you see, our duty this morning is just in a few words to try and examine the various voices of God and see whether that be true or not.

For instance, for I never like to leave this out, I suppose most of us this morning would say that God talked to them in nature. In this beautiful world, thrilling from the grave in the revival light again, I hope you have all got enough of a receiving set within you to hear God talk to you in nature. Of course, without that we never would have any science. If I can take up a book and read it and understand it, it means that behind that book there is a mind kindred to my own. And if science can read the book of nature—that is exactly what it does, we dwell not in a chaos but in a cosmos —if science can read the book of nature, then there is a mind behind it cognate and kindred to our own. I wonder why it is, if you were out in a great storm and in peril of shipwreck, you would immediately feel you were a sinner. I wonder why it is when you walk over the moors of Arran every bird and every beast flies from you in dread, the game birds and the hares and the rabbits and the deer fly from you in dread. Is not there something wrong? Has not some

harmony been broken ? Do you think God
ever intended that ? Now I do not say anything about the pain you feel when you are
confronted with perfect beauty. I do not say
anything of the song of birds that, as Burns
says, 'Ye 'll brak my heart' ; but what I do
say is, even in the dim voices of nature God
does not only say, ' Child, am not I beautiful ? '
but God says, ' Child, you have broken something, you are a sinner.'

Then does not God talk to you in conscience ?
Don't you all just believe with me this morning
that in the still small voice of conscience God is
talking to you ? I beg of you never to give up
that faith. People are discussing conscience
to-day, talking about the evolution of the conscience, how we have got it from the instinct of
the herd or from the first people who gathered
together into a community. A thing is not
what it came from ; a thing is what it has the
capacity to become, and therefore, for all your
study, and it is a beautiful study, never forget
that conscience is just God talking to you to-day.
If your conscience is not dead, and it is dead
in some people, seared with a hot iron, what
does it say to you ? Does it say, ' Child, your
temptation was too strong for you, therefore
you are not guilty ' ? Does it say, ' Child,
these are dreadful circumstances you live in,

therefore you are not guilty'? Does it say, 'Child, it is all heredity, and the blame rests on your grandfather'? It says, 'Child, you are guilty.' It says to you, 'Whatever your temptation or heredity, *you* are guilty ; nobody else.' And if you say you have not sinned, that you could not help it, that things were too strong for you, that you were in the hands of a determined fate, don't you see you make God a liar whenever He talks to you in conscience ?

Then I hope everybody here this morning agrees with me that God speaks to us in the Old Testament. You know, I do not envy the man who does not hear God speaking to him in the Old Testament. Somebody has said the day is coming when we are all going to be divided, not into Anglicans and Presbyterians, but into people who see and people who do not see. But I would rather put it this way : we are going all to be divided into people who hear and people who do not hear. Now I don't care one straw what view you take of the Old Testament. You can believe in its verbal inspiration if you like ; you can rejoice, as I rejoice, in all the great results of the higher criticism ; but the point is, what do you hear in the Old Testament ? Do you hear the voice of God to you ? Well now, if you do, that whole utterance is based upon the reality of sin and nothing else, except God Himself willing to forgive it. You take the story of the Fall : God telling a little story to His poor children and bringing in old elements like talking serpents. What is at the back of it ? That sin is real, that guilt is real, that the fear that follows guilt is real, and that is the very meaning. Then you have got the sacrifices of smoke at these Jewish altars, you have got the forty years' wandering in the wilderness, you have got the seventy years' exile in Babylon, and you have got the anguish of the Psalmist that we read this morning, and you have got the trumpet cry of the Prophet, that He is the Lord God who forgiveth sin. Then you say sin is no reality, it does not exist, it is only a negative. You make God a liar in the whole utterance of the Old Testament. Don't you see ?

Then far above the Old Testament, have not we got the New Testament, and I who know a little about Plato and Dante and Shakespeare never hesitate a moment to call the New Testament the most wonderful book in the world. Written by men of strong individuality, each of them with his own angle and his own outlook, each with his own type of theology, each with his own aspect of the Lord, and yet all of them banded together as with a

band of steel in this one conviction, that man
needs redemption, and that God in His mercy
is willing to give it now. You get so tired of
books whose only parrot-cry is, Educate, educate, educate ; books that tell you that give
time to our human race and it will evolve
into a kind of superman. The New Testament comes to you and me and says, ' Child,
first of all there is a barrier between you and
God, and that barrier has got to be taken out
of the way.' In other words, you do not want
to be reformed, you need to be born again,
and then you can start educating and evolving.
The whole New Testament is based on this,
that you and I are guilty sinful creatures, and if
you come along and say, ' We have not sinned,'
—you know, I have read a book or two costing
a shilling, and they tell me that sin is just a
fiction of the priest—you are making God a
liar as He speaks to us in the New Testament.

And then, of course, the whole argument
comes to its height in this : God in His infinite mercy has talked and spoken to you and
me in our blessed Lord and Saviour Jesus
Christ. ' In the beginning was the Word, and
the Word was with God, and the Word (the
expression of the thought—the Oratio against
the Ratio) became flesh and dwelt among us.'
' His name shall be called Jesus.' Why ?

Because he is a beautiful teacher, because He is our example, because He is a great social leader ? 'His name shall be called Jesus because He saves His people from their sins.' There were things that our blessed Lord made very light of, things that He did not care a straw for, and sometimes they mean everything to us ; but there was one thing our Lord never made light of, deepened it, intensified it all the time, and that was the fact of human sin. It was that which brought Him here ; it was that which sent Him among the publicans and sinners ; it was that that nailed Him to the cross. And if you venture to say, 'I have not sinned,' 'It was not sin at all,' 'Sin does not exist,' don't you make Him just a liar when He talks to us in the Lord Jesus Christ ? I beg of you not to do it. Life is far too serious for that. To wrap yourself up in excuses is to be naked before the great white throne. It is far better just to say this morning, however humbling it is, 'God be merciful to me, a sinner.' 'Seek ye the Lord while He may be found, call ye upon Him while He is near. Let the wicked forsake his way and the unrighteous man his thought, and let him return unto the Lord, and He will have mercy upon him, and to our God, for He will abundantly pardon.'

IF we suppose for a moment that those chapters of Genesis which give us the story of Abraham's life were to be cut out from the Bible, we may be sure that an intense curiosity about this Abraham would soon possess every reader of the Scripture. As a traveller climbing the mountain-side looks down from the height he has gained upon some valley and catches glimpses there of a strong river whose waters flow from a source he cannot see, so through the pastures of the Word of God there flows increasingly the influence of Abraham, until the hastiest observer becomes curious to learn where that river has its rise. We find the name of Abraham in the Psalms. He is often referred to by the Prophets. The martyr Stephen had him in his thoughts. He moves through the glowing arguments of Paul. Fourteen or fifteen times in the New Testament you will find the name of Abraham introduced, not incidentally, but as a name of paramount authority. I need not remind you what he meant to Christ, nor how often Christ cited him in teaching. Some of the most notable sayings of our Lord recall and centre in this patriarch. Who, then, was this man of dim antiquity, whose influence was so lasting and so powerful that every writer of the Holy Scriptures is ready to bow in reverence at his feet ?

And if, from a study of the Bible, we ask in wondering interest who Abraham was, much more shall we ask it when we enlarge our view, and take a larger survey of the world's history. Not only do Protestants and Roman Catholics and the Greek Church unite in their common reverence for Abraham, but far beyond the bounds of Christendom, and where the name of Jesus is anathema, there are millions of our fellow-men who are at one with us in our homage to the father of the faithful. There are but three great religions in the world that cherish the truth of the one and only God. These three are the religions of the Christian, and of the Jew, and of the Moham-medan. And as three rivers that flow far apart may, for all that, be born of the same spring, so Christian and Jew and Moslem derive from Abraham as from a common ancestor. Wherever yesterday in Europe or in Asia the Jews assembled to worship in their synagogues, wherever in India or Africa to-day the Moslem is bowing at the call to prayer, there the name of Abraham is reverenced. The Christian knight who rode to the Crusade, and the Saracen who set his lance to drive him back ; the Shylock who was baited by the rabble, and the rabble who wrecked their hate on Shylock ; the Sultan of Turkey who massacred the Armenians, and the Armenians whom he did to death—all had a common ancestor in Abraham. Who, then, was Abraham ? Who was this mighty figure ? Who was the man who for four thousand years had held a spiritual place unparalleled ? To all these questions the answer must be found in the original story of the Book of Genesis. And to that story, for some few coming Sabbaths, I wish to invite your thought.

Abraham was born in Ur of the Chaldees. He was a child of the land of Chaldea. If you will consult your map you will see that Chaldea stretches northward from the Persian Gulf, and consists of that alluvial country which is watered by the Tigris and Euphrates. To-day it is a land of desolation, of dreary and monotonous levels of sand. Here one may see the tents of wandering Arabs, and there a cluster of miserable huts, but such are the only signs of life to-day where once there was a teeming population, and where the harvests were so luxuriously plentiful as to excite the wonder of the world. It was so in the time of Herodotus, the Greek historian, whose travels had taken him to that distant quarter. And he hesitates to say how rich the crops were lest folk should think it was a traveller's tale. Yet it was so even in his day, and still more markedly so four thousand years ago, when the literature of Greece was still unwritten and the majesty of Rome was still unborn. Tablets and monuments have told their secret now. Libraries have been unearthed, and read. Explorers have been at work in these waste places, with a rich reward for their courageous patience. And now to-day, dimly as in a glass, we may see the Chaldea in which Abraham lived, and know something of that human life on which his boyish eyes would look so eagerly. We see the plains covered with crops of wheat. We see the beauty of the date-palm everywhere. Here on the hillside are the sunny vineyards. There in the village is the sound of looms. And everywhere we can discern the brickmakers, working in the clay which was abundant, for Chaldea had no building stone save such as was carried by water from a distance. There were no forests such as that on Lebanon, no cedar trees that would make beams and joists. But along by the margin of its many waters there was the whispering of gigantic reeds. And these were cut and hardened in the sun and skilfully enwrought among the bricks, where to-day they still lie strong and tough in the ruins of palace and of temple. Such were the arts and crafts of that old people, nor are traces wanting of the higher studies. The science of government was studied, so was law; so, with notable ardour, was astronomy. Chaldea was the home of those wise men who were led to the manger at Bethlehem by a star, heralds of all those whose way to Christ has lain along the road of earnest toil.

Now the slightest acquaintance with history will tell us that a life like that is sure to create cities, and we are therefore prepared to hear that there were cities in the Chaldea of Abraham's day. Here and there amid the waste of sand are certain mounds of artificial origin. Many of these have now been dug into, under the supervision of explorers. And there have been discovered ancient streets, and the ruins of palace and of cottage and temple-floors that in that distant age were worn by the passing of a thousand feet. Of these cities the capital was Ur, the city where Abraham was born. To-day it is several miles from the sea-coast, but it was not so four thousand years

ago. For age by age the Tigris and Euphrates
have been carrying seaward a vast mass of
soil, and driving the ocean always further back.
In the time of Abraham, Ur was a seaport.
It lay on the margin of the Persian Gulf.
Her harbour was a busy scene of traffic, and
ships were there from Arabia and Africa. Ur
was familiar with the stir and movement, the
mingling of nationalities and speech, the difference of colour and of dress that are characteristic of a port. Here Abraham was born. Here
was his boyhood spent. Here were passed
his impressionable years. He was no child of
solitary places, nursing his heart in loneliness
and silence. His was no infancy like that at
Nazareth, where the village slept amid the
quiet hills. He was a city boy, familiar with
the streets, and that is significant of much.

Of the religion of this ancient land not a
little has now come to light, and being the
faith in which Abraham was bred, the slightest
detail of it can never lose its interest. It was
a worship of the powers of nature, personified
as male and female gods. At the head of all
there was one mighty god, the last survival of
a purer faith ; but the deities who filled the
people's thought, and were the objects of their
daily worship, were the gods and goddesses of
sun and moon and stars. In Ur it was the

moon-god who was reverenced. There was a mighty temple to her honour there. Around her had already gathered many legends whose echoes may be heard in Greek mythology. And such was the importance of Ur, and the fame of her temple to the moon, that the worship which was celebrated there seems to have influenced the whole land of Chaldea. What the moral issues of this worship were it is not easy for us now to say. From the analogy of the Greek worship of Diana we might conceive it to have been far from elevating. And the one fact that Abraham was inspired to leave the city, and become an exile, is a divine indictment of its tenor. Clearly the moral atmosphere of Ur was not congenial to a life of faith. It was no place for such an one as Abraham, whose heart was thirsty for the living God. He had to leave it at the call of heaven that he might become the father of the faithful, and that one fact is ominous for Ur.

As was to be looked for, a world of story has gathered round the early years of Abraham. It is to be found in the Talmud of the Jews, and in the Koran, the sacred book of the Mohammedans. The Bible is silent on that life in Ur, as it is silent on the life in Nazareth. It draws a veil over those earlier years when character was forming in the home. But just as there has gathered a literature around the infancy and youth of Christ, so in the writings of Moslem and of Jew there is a wealth of legend about Abraham. Is it all legend? Is it all fable? Are there embodied in these ancient stories no elements of truth, that fathers had passed on to sons through countless generations? It is perhaps impossible to tell. This only we can say, that when we strip away the foolish miracles and search for the plain prose beneath that Eastern poetry, we find the traces of a character so brave and pure that it might well be that of youthful Abraham. We see a youth enthusiastic for the right, and nobly intolerant of what is wrong. We see a heart so sensitively pure that it recoils in abhorrence from idolatry. We see a will so resolute, a mind so nimble, a wisdom so discerning and pervasive, that it is difficult to believe that all these stories are baseless and unsupported fancies. Let me tell you two of these legends that may be taken as typical of all. Both are from the pages of the Talmud.

The first is that when Abraham was a lad he broke all the idols of his father's house, broke them all except the biggest of them, into whose hands he put the club. When his father came home he was intensely angry, and he asked Abraham who had broken his·gods. And Abraham answered, 'Is not that the culprit ?' pointing to the great idol with the club. 'How can a man-made idol do such things ?' asked Terah. Whereupon Abraham instantly replied, 'My father, if an idol cannot do even *that*, do you think it is wise of you to worship them ?'

The other tells that Abraham was long imprisoned, but at last he won his liberty again. And looking up at the expanse of heaven he asked himself, 'Who is the maker of all that ?' First the sun rose in his unclouded splendour, and Abraham fell down before it and adored. But evening came and the sun sank from sight, and Abraham cried, 'This cannot be the Creator, for this is subject to extinction.' Then the moon rose and the host of stars appeared, and still Abraham was gazing heavenwards. And he cried, 'Surely the moon is the mistress of the universe, and the stars the mighty throng of her attendants.' But even as he gazed the moon was setting and the stars were growing fainter at the dawn, and Abraham was left without his god. Then he arose and cried, 'These are but creatures. They move in obedience to some mightier power. Some hand unseen is ordering their course, and at His ordering they move as messengers.' So Abraham lifted up his heart to God, the mighty and invisible Creator. Him only from that hour he worshipped. Before Him, and Him only, would he bow.

Now granting, as we grant at once, that this is imaginative oriental poetry, is there not that in it which forms a fitting background for all we know of the character of Abraham? Four hundred years had elapsed since the Flood, and in these centuries the heavens had been of brass. No messenger of God had come to men. No voice had broken the silence of the sky. And in these centuries men had forgotten God, and wandered into the worship of His creatures, and fallen from the adoration of the highest into the worship of sun and moon and star. Such was the world then. Such was Chaldea. Such was the religion of the Urites. But God, who hath never left Himself without a witness, had here and there a heart that was His own. Touched by the Spirit that moveth where He will, breathed on in secret by the breath of God, such was Abraham in a godless city and in the bosom of a godless home. On a still summer evening, when scarce a breath is stirring, all trees save one are motionless. The oak is still. The ash droops silently.

Even the graceful birch forgets to sway. Only
the aspen makes a quick response, and rustles
and quivers like a living thing. Only the
aspen answers to the breath that appeals in-
audibly to all. So was it in that dark and evil
world. The Spirit of God was breathing on
mankind. It touched a thousand hearts in
gentle ministry, yet only here and there a
heart responded. And of these hearts that
quivered in the breeze the greatest was the
heart of Abraham. He broke through all the
trammels of idolatry in his thirst for the living
God.

We may therefore picture Abraham at Ur,
and probably we shall be very near the truth.
We may picture him as breaking with idolatry,
and worshipping the one and living God.
Everything in his birthplace was against him.
The powers of idolatry were all opposed to
him. All the culture and learning of his city
was based on a superstition he rejected. He
was quite certain to provoke hostility. He
was equally certain to suffer persecution.
Nor was Abraham the kind of man to flinch
from the necessary consequences of his creed.
Probably his sorest trial of all was the estrangement there would be at home. His father and
his brethren worshipped idols, and Abraham
had to take his stand against them all. And

that is always a sore thing to do, especially
when there is love at home and tender memories of happy days when childhood was well
guarded and content. Through it all, Abraham trusted God. He had it in his heart
that God would save him. Unknown and
young, he laid deep the foundation of the
massive character of after years. And how
that character enriched and deepened under
the gracious leadership of God shall be our
endeavour to portray in the lectures of the
coming Sabbaths.

1. ATTENTIVE students will have observed how markedly the Bible is a book of calls. It is a long record of the call of God, summoning man to obedience and to service. The kind of contact between the divine and human is always determinative of a sacred book. It is that which gives it its peculiar character, and in the long-run its spiritual value. Let it be noted that in our Bible the contact is of one unvarying kind ; it is the contact of the voice of God with the spirit and the heart of man. God forces nobody into His service. He never batters down the human will. He speaks with the authority of heaven, yet with the accent of reason and of love. And it is by listening to this heavenly voice, and responding to it in an act of faith, that men are everywhere throughout the Scripture honoured with the service of the Highest. Samuel was called when he was but a child ; Moses when he was well advanced in years ; Isaiah was called in the stillness of the Temple, and Matthew amid the traffic of his business. The place and

circumstances are but secondary. They are varied as human life is varied. The one unchanging element is this, that service is based upon a summons. To-day, then, in our course of lectures we come on one of the most notable of calls. It is notable not only in itself but in its influence upon the world. 'Now the Lord said unto Abraham, Get thee out of thy country, and from thy kindred, and from thy father's house, unto a land that I will shew thee.'

2. Now it is to be noted that according to Genesis, our one authority upon the subject, this call was not given to Abraham in Ur; it was given to him in Haran. Ur, as we saw in our last lecture, was the city where Abraham was born and grew to manhood. Haran lay a long way to the north on the left bank of the Euphrates. And according to Genesis it was not Abraham, it was Terah, the father of Abraham, who took the step of quitting Ur and travelling to this new locality. Why he did it the Scripture does not tell us, but with tolerable certainty we may conjecture it. Terah was of the race of Shem, who were always lovers of the open world. The spirit of cities was not in his blood—as it was in the builders of the race of Ham—and though his lot was cast in busy Ur, his heart was always hungry for the country. Wordsworth tells us,

in one of his short poems, of a country maiden
who came up to London. And there one day
above the crowded street she heard the singing
of a captive skylark. And in a moment her
heart was in the country and there was a river
flowing down Cheapside ; and such, I take it,
had been Terah's vision, as he moved among
the crowds of Ur. Whatever was his motive,
can we not discover in it now the hand of
God ? Was it not easier for Abraham to hear
His call in the quiet of Haran than in the
noise of Ur ? Amid the distracting influences
of the city it might have been hard to catch
the still small voice, but it was not so hard
where there was peace, and the brooding quietness of nature. Moses was taken from Egyptian
glitter into the loneliness of desert places.
Samuel was taken from his noisy playmates
into the stillness of the house of God. And
so was Abraham taken out of Ur that he
might catch the voice in quiet Haran, and he
was so taken by his father. Such is the unconscious influence of a father upon the spirit
and welfare of his children. He moves his
dwelling to another place, and it may be he
is altering their destiny. Even a simple thing
like change of residence may have mighty
issues in the children's history, and always,
therefore, should be a time of prayer and of

quiet supplication of God's blessing. We cannot bring our families to Christ. It takes a mightier power than man to effect that. But we can all do consciously what Terah did unconsciously : we can make it easier for them to hear the call. We can so live before them every day, so help them to fall in love with what is good, that they will be ready to receive the voice, and Ur shall be transfigured into Haran.

3. Again, it is notable that the call of Abraham began the divine method of election. In that light, therefore, it is well to look at it, when we think of all that election was to mean. Roughly speaking, four centuries had gone since God had sent the judgment of the Flood. No message had come from heaven in these centuries. No voice had broken the silence of the sky. And all the time men had been travelling downward, away from the knowledge of the living God, till faith was dead and reverence was gone and character was vicious and depraved. It was then that God intervened again. It was then He showed His love for human kind. It was then He revealed those purposes of grace that were to be crowned in the Lord Jesus Christ. And what we can never ponder on too deeply is the method which God

adopted in His love : 'And the Lord said
unto Abraham, Get thee out from thy country,
and from thy father's house.' Not to the lost
world did the Lord speak, although His love
went out to all the world. Not to the crowds
who thronged the city streets, though every
member of that crowd was precious to Him.
He chose one man ; to him God spake ; with
him He made a start ; from him the blessing
was to flow to all. Abraham was not elected for
his own sake merely. He was elected for the
sake of others. If others were passed by and
he was chosen, it was not that God was heedless of others. God had a purpose of mercy
to them all, nor was it His will that one of
them should perish ; the burden of the world
was on His heart when He elected One to
hear His voice. If a great river had no con-
fining bank, and if it were suffered to spread
where'er it pleased, how soon its waters would
be sapped and lost over the surface of a thousand
fields. But that same river, bound to the one
channel, and held in narrowest and strictest
compass, will bring enrichment to the land
it waters and build up the prosperity of cities.
Brethren, when we think about election, let
us remember that it is like that river. How
many of our harsh thoughts would flee away,
if we only conceived of it like that. Election

is no arbitrary choice of a capricious and un-heeding God. It is the loving method of the Father for winning the widest blessings for mankind.

4. Let it be noted again in regard to Abra-ham's action that outwardly it was not peculiar or exceptional. On the surface of it, it did not differ greatly from what one might have seen in many quarters. There are ages which are marked by a great fixity, in which there is but little racial movement. There are others when life seems to be fluid, and everywhere is movement and migration. And such was the period in which Abraham lived, a period of unrest and of unsettlement, when every-where men were on the move and pushing forward to the unknown. As the race grew this was inevitable. Expansion was a necessity of life. At the original centres of the race there came to be overcrowding, and starvation. And so, for room to live and food to eat and pas-turage for cattle and for sheep, swarm after swarm of the human family had migrated out to the broad world. Outwardly the move-ment of Abraham and his clan was but another of these tribal wanderings. He was not the first and he was not the last who had boldly set his face to the unknown. And when the watchman on the Damascus walls descried the

string of camels in the distance, to him it would just mean another chieftain smit with the roving passion of the times.

5. But the point to note is that the migration of Abraham was not like that. Outwardly it bore a common aspect, inwardly it was unparalleled. There was no necessity for Abraham going, for at Haran there was pasture in abundance. There was food and plenty in these river lands ; and even then Abraham was prosperous. And then, remember he was no longer young ; he was seventy-five years old when he departed : he had reached a time when the craving for adventure had taken to itself wings and fled away. To most men, as they get older, change becomes increasingly distasteful. They cling to what they know and what they love. They are dependent on familiar comforts. It was no love of change that mastered Abraham, then, when he crossed Euphrates and journeyed to the west. It was a motive that was unknown to others. Other chieftains had everything to gain. Abraham had everything to lose. Other chieftains were consulting self. Abraham was obeying God. He was only doing what other men were doing, in a time of continuous emigration, but he was doing it in such a spirit as sets him apart for evermore.

6. Brethren, as it is with Abraham, so is it with the Christian to-day. It is not the thing he does that is unique : it is the motive that inspires him when he does it. Think of the missionary who goes to the heart of Africa. Is there anything unparalleled in that ? Are there not trading-stations all around him, with young men there who have gone out from home ? Think of the worker in the city slum. Is he the only stranger who is found there ? If the district offered a good business opening, would there not be twenty who would seize on it ? Ah, sirs, it is not the thing itself that is unique, it is not the outward act that is unparalleled : it is the spirit in which the thing is done, the motive with which the action is performed. Two actions may be outwardly alike, yet in the sight of God how diverse they may be. To the eyes of men there may be little difference, to the eyes of heaven the difference of worlds. For the one may be an action of self-interest, inspired by thoughts of personal advancement, while in the other a man may be aflame with an unselfish and divine idea. That is the heroism of the Christian faith. It is not the heroism of achievement merely. It is the heroism of the inward spirit that seeks the will of God in common things. It holds by the ideal

in the usual, it strives to trace the rainbow through the rain, it emigrates as other chiefs are doing, but it does it at the call of God.

7. Now in the Epistle to the Hebrews, as you know, this act of Abraham is an act of faith. It is regarded there as one of the mightiest instances that man has ever given of faith in God. Will you allow me, then, in closing to point out to you how the faith of Abraham was shown? There are things we should observe.

8. In the first place, it was by faith that Abraham recognised the voice of God. How Abraham was called we do not know. We say, with the Scripture, that God spake to him. But do you think that because God spake to him, no faith was needed on the part of Abraham? You may be sure of this, that never hath God spoken to man so as to crush and overwhelm the man and force him in despite of his own will. So God may speak to sunshine and to storm when He commands them forth to do His bidding. So God may speak to creatures of the field when they obey their instincts and are happy. But to man, made in His own image, able to think His thoughts and know His love, God never hath spoken thus and never will. Always there is the response of personality, the character that

is fitted to receive. Always there is the ear
that has been trained by listening for the
worthiest and the best. And so the very fact
that Abraham hearkened and knew it was the
Lord who was addressing him is like a window
opened on his character, or a silent proclama-
tion of his faith. Other voices had appealed
to Abraham. He knew the charm and glamour
of idolatry. Not once or twice the priests of
Ur had told him that they had received
messages from heaven. And now, among all
the voices that appealed—and voices, some of
them of tender memory—Abraham recognised
the voice of God, and in that recognition there
was faith. As it was with Abraham, so is it
with you and me to-day. God will not force
you into acquiescence ; there must be faith to
answer when He calls. To hear Him amid
our trials, that is faith ; to hear Him amid
our questionings is faith ; to hear His voice,
in such an age as this, is possible to faith and
faith alone.

9. In the second place, he showed his faith
by his obedience. Abraham did not only hear,
he acted. Once convinced it is the voice of
God, and Abraham is starting on his journey.
Probably behind his great resolve there is
much hidden that we shall never know. It
is very likely that the will of God only became

gradually clear.   There would be a gradual
wakening of conscience, a feeling that a hand
was beckoning, a growing insistency of daily
providences all converging on one point.
Through many a doubt Abraham may have
passed, waiting for the clearing of God's will.
For years he may have prayed and watched
and waited, uncertain of the leadership of
heaven.   But the point to note is that when
at last God spoke, when the broken syllables
united into speech, then Abraham instantly
obeyed.   He was no longer young, as I have
said.   He had rooted deep in the quiet life at
Haran.   There were tender memories to make
it dear, too, for was not his father sleeping in
the sod ?   And spite of everything, Abraham
obeyed, because he was certain it was the will
of God.   And it is in that that the writer of
the Hebrews finds his instance of heroic faith.
God grant that we may sometimes show our
faith in loyal and unquestioning obedience.
It is when we do what may be hard to do, and
do it because we are certain it is right, that
God is able, out of stony ground, to raise up
children unto Abraham.

10. In the third place, Abraham's faith was
shown in his confidence that there was a better
country.   He never doubted that beyond the
sun there was a place unseen which was pre-

pared for him. You must bear in mind the
ignorance of Abraham. He knew nothing
whatever of the promised land. It was liter-
ally a land for him from whose bourne no
traveller returned. How different from the
emigrant to-day who, though his journey be
ten thousand miles, may have his map with
every village on it and all the information
to his hand. Then think of the direction he
was sent in. Did God direct him to the sunny
south ? Did the finger of heaven point him
to the east, the region of sunrise and of hope ?
Not so. He was directed to the west, he had
to travel towards the setting sun ; he had to
turn his back upon the dawn, when he crossed
Euphrates for the desert. He went out not
knowing whither he went. The world was all
before him where to choose. He crossed the
river that was swift and strong and parted him
from old familiar faces. And this was the
triumph of the faith of Abraham, that going
out on that untrodden path he yet believed
there was a better country which God had
prepared for those who loved Him.

11. Brethren, as it was with Abraham, so is
it with you and me to-day. " Faith is the sub-
stance of things hoped for, the evidence of
things not seen." " Eye hath not seen and ear
hath never heard the things that God hath

prepared for those who love Him." No reasoning can ever prove to us the certainty of a blessed immortality. But we believe through Jesus Christ our Lord that for us and for the dear ones whom we loved, beyond the river there is a better country where sorrow and sighing shall have fled away. We, too, are not summoned to the east. We are ever stepping westward to the sunset. And we have to part with many a cherished thing, and lose for a season the familiar faces. But we believe, through Jesus Christ our Lord, that beyond these voices there is peace. We believe, through Jesus Christ our Lord, that sundered lives shall be reknit again. Yes, we believe, through Jesus Christ our Lord, that there is a brighter and a better land where in unclouded love there shall be joy, and in perfect service shall be rest.

IN obedience to the call of God, Abraham went forth to the promised land, and it is in the hour of that obedience that his pilgrim life begins. There is a sense in which every man (whatever his beliefs) is a pilgrim and a stranger on the earth. We are here at the longest but for a little time, and our tenure of what we have is fleeting. But there is a peculiar and especial sense in which the Godward life is a pilgrimage, and it is with Abraham that that life begins. When the pilgrims, in the *Pilgrim's Progress*, come to Vanity Fair, you remember the three things which struck the citizens. The first was the dress which the pilgrims wore. The second was the kind of speech they used. But the third and most notable, says Bunyan, was this : that the pilgrims set very light by all their wares, and would not so much as look at them. All these marks might have been seen in Abraham, and very notably the last. He had set light by much that is dear to men when he went forth at the call of God. He had left his home, with his ancestral ties, and the memories that now clustered richly round it, and left it at an age when most men are setting their minds chiefly on repose.

Yet we must not think, though that be true, that Abraham thought lightly of this present world. It was no part of his obedience to God to be dead to present ties and opportunities. It has been urged sometimes against the religious life that it withdraws a man from present service. Fixing his gaze upon another world, it makes him callous to the claims of this one. But however true that charge may be of some who have denied their burden that they might live with God, it certainly was far from true of Abraham. The very fact that he took his family with him is a sign of the depth and strength of his affections. The very fact of his increasing wealth is a sign that he never neglected his day's work. And over and over again, in Canaan, we find him acting as only a man could act who was intensely alive to present duty and to the summons of the ties of home. We have but to remember how he fought for Lot, when Lot had been made a prisoner of war. We have but to remember how he pled for Lot, when Lot was in peril of his life in Sodom. We have but to remember that, and we shall feel that Abraham, though in the noblest sense a pilgrim, was never insensible to present duty or to the urgency of present claims. It is always a travesty of true religion when it withdraws a man from duty. The pilgrim spirit means a loose hold of much, but it never means a light and heedless heart. On the contrary, he who is travelling God-ward, with a deep sense that he is here a stranger, is the man of all men who must be most alive to the social needs of his own day. When Daniel, a prisoner in Babylon, opened his windows towards Jerusalem, the thousand voices on the streets of Babylon would be far louder than with a closed casement. And so, when the windows of the heart are opened on things that are unseen and eternal, the calls of the life around us are not deadened, rather they are louder than before. All social effort runs back to religion. It is in religion that it is born. It was so with Abraham. It was so with Jesus. It has been so all through the years of Christendom. And nothing is of worse omen for to-morrow than the attempt which we see made to-day to dissociate the service of humanity from the service and the sense of God.

It is notable, again, how silent the Scriptures are on all the incidents of Abraham's journey. They went forth to go into the land of Canaan, we read, and into the land of Canaan they

came. When we open a book of travels to-
day, you know how fully the journey is described. You know how graphically it is all
described, often with photographs of strange
and dangerous places. But in this pilgrimage
there are no details. Nothing is told us of
what was borne or suffered. They set out to
go to the land of Canaan, and into the land
of Canaan they came. It is not difficult to
reconstruct that journey over a wild and inhospitable waste. It was not the easy passage
of a day. It was a passage of toilsome and
laborious weeks. When Laban followed that
route, pursuing Jacob, it took him a week to
make up on Jacob, and for Abraham, with his
retainers and his herds, it would be far more
tedious than that. It was a journey of the
utmost difficulty. It was a journey of no little
peril. We shall never know what hairbreadth
escapes there were, what hours when the heart
had almost fainted. Yet on all that the Word
of God is silent. It tells us Abraham's aim,
and his accomplishment. It tells us quietly
that he set forth and, trusting God, came to
his journey's end. That quiet and assured
confidence is one of the outstanding marks
of Scripture. It never contemplates, from first
to last, that a man who really seeks God
should fail. It touches with a light hand on

stress and peril, not because stress and peril
are awanting, but because it knows that when
faith makes its venture, none can pluck out
of the Father's hand.   Let a man aim at anything less than God, and he is always liable
to disappointment.   Let him set his heart on
a lower than the highest, and for all his effort
he may miss it.   It is not by aiming too high
that men are baffled.   They are baffled when
they aim too low.   He never said to any of
the seed of Jacob ' Seek ye Me ' in vain.   One
of the great Hebrew words for sin means,
at the root of it, to miss the mark.   Is not
that what sin is always doing in the world—
missing the mark the heart is set upon ?   But
he that aims at God never does that.   ' Blessed
are they that hunger and thirst after righteousness.'   They set forth to go to the land of
Canaan, and into the land of Canaan they
came.

There are, says Browning,

> ' Two points in the adventure of the diver,
>   One, when a beggar, he prepares to plunge,
>   One, when a prince, he rises with his pearl.'

And so, in the life of faith, there are two
points ; and it is on these the Scripture dwells,
one when faith launches out into the deep, and
the other when that faith is crowned in God.

Now, it is not difficult for us, as we look backwards, to see what a fitting land this land of Canaan was. All that we know to-day of Palestine justified the ways of God to man. No country could have been more singularly suited for such a task as Abraham was called to. No country could have been better fitted for the spiritual discipline of Israel. And that principally for the following reason. Palestine is one of the most central of all lands, and yet one of the most secluded of all lands. It lay in the very heart of the old world, with the great states on every side of it. And yet, though central, it was strangely isolated, washed on the one hand by the sea, and on the other bordered by the desert, itself an inhospitable sea of sand. Round it were Babylonia and Assyria, Persia, Phœnicia and Egypt. It was in touch with that great and busy world, for the great routes of traffic passed beside it. Yet all the time it lay in isolation, separated from the other kingdoms, able to keep in touch with other nations, yet also to be independent of them all. It was not a great country. It was the least of all lands. It could never hope to fight with mighty monarchies. It was a singularly fertile land, yet liable to be overwhelmed by storm and earthquake. And all this, as it is clear to us to-day, reveals to us the choice of divine wisdom, in making such a land the home of Abraham, and the place where Israel was to worship God. There they could pursue their way in peace, and learn their shepherding of the unseen. There, with the spiritual truth that was their mission, they could go forth and be a blessing to mankind. It was to such a land that Abraham was brought when he went out not knowing whither he went, when he set his face towards his desert journey, and trusted the issues of it to his God. He had no previous knowledge of the land. Even when he reached it, he did not know it. God had to tell him, under the oak at Sichem, that this was the country he was to inherit. Yet who can fail to see in that selection the working of a purpose more than human? who can fail to see that, step by step, Abraham was led to his appointed place? That is always the reward of faith, when it goes forward in obedient trust. All the light it gets is for one step. All the guidance it gets is for to-day. Yet faith will always discover in the end that it was not wandering idly in the desert, but slowly, and oftentimes circuitously, was being led to the prepared place. Think of the Pilgrim Fathers, for example, when at the bidding of conscience they left England. Like Abraham, were they not going to the unknown, to a savage and inhospitable shore? Yet who does not know that God was in that choice, and had determined the bounds of their habitation, and was leading them into that very country where they might be a blessing to mankind? God does not let us see where we are going. The all-important thing is the direction. If moment by moment we are true to Him, the land of promise may be left in His hands. The one thing certain is that we shall reach it, and find in it an ample preparation, and learn at last, just as Abraham learned, that it is the place appointed for our service.

Yet, while all that is clear to us to-day, it may not have been so clear to Abraham. It is very probable that, reaching Canaan, his first feeling was one of disappointment. Think of it, he had left his Chaldean home that he might have liberty to worship God. He had shaken off from him, he hoped for ever, the associations of a vile idolatry. And yet, when he reached the land that God had given him, the Canaanite was then in the land, and all that was worst in the vile rites of heathendom was known and practised by these very Canaanites. Of course, you are not to think of Canaan as being the Canaan which Joshua found. The land was not crowded then, and full of cities, as it was when Joshua led back the Israelites. But it was crowded enough to have Gomorrah in it. And it was bad enough to have Sodom in it. And for a man whose heart was hungering for God, Sodom and Gomorrah were enough. It was not merely that these towns were wicked. They were wicked because of their religion. Here, in the land that God had called him to, were the very iniquities that he had known at home. And what I say is, that seeing that corruption and all the abominations which it sanctioned, do you not think that the heart of Abraham sank, as if all his pilgrimage had been in vain? It is very notable that just then we read for the first time that God appeared. Hitherto the Lord had spoken to Abraham. Now we read, the Lord appeared to Abraham. And though we may not fathom what that means, for no man hath seen God at any time, yet at least it means that in the hour of peril the sense of the living God was overwhelming. It is not always when one is setting out that the perils of pilgrimage are worst. There is a buoyancy of heart in all beginnings, especially for a great soul like Abraham. The sorest peril is ofttimes near the end, when hopes long cherished seem to be disappointed, when all that a man has striven for in faithfulness seems to be so differ-

ent from his dream. That, I take it, was the
mood of Abraham when he first halted under
the oak of Sichem. He had left everything
to shun idolatry, and here was an oak tree
reeking with its practices. And then, says
Scripture, God appeared to Abraham—came
nearer to him than He had ever been—
brooded upon him with such a sense of blessing
that Abraham took courage and was strong.
We need our revelations not only at the beginnings of our journeys, we need them when we
have long been travelling, and when the
pilgrimage is nearly over. And often it is
then that they are richest and fullest of benediction and of heaven, and flood the soul
with such a sense of God that everything else
shrinks and becomes little. Depend upon it,
that when God speaks once God will always
speak again. If you have heard His voice and
have obeyed, it will not be silence thereafter
to the end. Nay, on the contrary, God will
appear to you, and be nearer in the hour of
disappointment than even in that most memorable hour when you first hearkened and
obeyed.

Now, that the faith of Abraham was greatly
strengthened by this new vision of God will
be apparent as we pursue his story. Let me
but point you to-day to two features which

characterise all his after-life.   In the first place,
whatever his temptations, Abraham never
sought to hurry God.   He had the quiet
strength to wait God's time, though waiting
must have been incredibly hard.   The land
was his, for God had given it to him.   It had
been made over to him in the promise.   God
had made clear to him time and again that
this new country was to be his kingdom.   Yet
to his dying day Abraham owned not a rood
of it.   He dwelt as a stranger in his own
possessions.   He built no dwelling-place as in
Chaldea.   He pitched his tent a day's march
nearer home.   Had he sought to conquer it
with the sword, it would have been quite
within his power to do so; for the only time
when Abraham took the sword, he was easily
and splendidly victorious.   But all such hasty
snatching at the promise was alien from his
simplicity of faith, and Abraham lived and
died a wanderer because of the splendour of
his trust in God.   When the mediæval mission-
aries went out into the wilderness, they had
one custom which was significant : when they
came to a forest which they had to fell, the
first tree that they felled they made a cross
of.   They were claiming all the wild for Jesus
Christ ;   they were marking it as part and
parcel of His Kingdom ;   they were taking

possession of it in the name of Jesus and un-
furling their banner of the Cross. In the same
way, Abraham built an altar. Wherever he
encamped he built an altar. It was not only
the gathering place for worship ; it was the
seal that all the land was God's. And yet in
that land Abraham lived and died, without
so much in it as would make a grave, and his
faith was as mighty in its quiet waiting as in
its instant and unquestioning obedience. It
is often the hardest of all tasks to wait, especially for eager and enthusiastic natures. It
was hard for Abraham and it was hard for
Christ, as we know from the temptation in
the wilderness. But faith must always be
ready for the long road ; it must learn to
be still and know that He is God. It must
believe that one day is as a thousand years
with God, and a thousand years as one day.

And then again, this reveals his faith, that
Abraham refused to leave the land. It was
always in his power to go back. He never
once dallied with the thought. He was seventy-
five years old when he reached Canaan. He
was a hundred and seventy-five when he died.
For a whole century he was a sojourner, far
from his kindred, far from his old home. Yet
if ever the longing touched him to return—
and it must have surged against his heart a

thousand times—Abraham rejected it and put it from him with a consistency of faith that was magnificent. Had everything gone prosperously with him, we might not have needed faith to explain that. But everything did not go prosperously with him—one of his first experiences was a famine. The grass withered in his fields, the water-courses were dried up and stony. His flocks and herds began to die of hunger, and all this in the land that God had given him. What visions would come to him, in such a season, of the abundance and luxuriance of Chaldea! How he would dream in the still night of Haran, where there had always been plenty and to spare! Yet through such seasons Abraham never faltered, never returned to what he had forsworn, never was mindful of the country he had left, though he had opportunity to have returned. There is a statue of General Gordon in London, which many of you must have seen. In it the sculptor has conceived of Gordon as looking for that help which never came. But there is another statue in Khartoum, and Gordon is not looking towards Egypt in it. He is looking away with brave and steady eyes to the desert that he had lived for and had loved. That was how Abraham set his eyes in Canaan. He endured as seeing God who is invisible. True to the vision he had had of God, he made his calling and election sure. And when we are tempted, as we often are, to fall back again on lower levels, tempted to give up what we have won and return to the habits or ways we have forsworn, it is then we should remember this great soul who was so simply and so bravely true, and who, when everything was dark and dreary, held to the highest he had seen.

THE student of Scripture is constantly impressed by its amazing and unfailing candour. It never condones a single human fault or palliates a single human weakness. The Bible is as a great gallery of heroes, yet it is ignorant of hero worship. It draws no veil across their hours of sin, nor does it shelter them when they are less than their true selves. It sets them in the clear light of reality that we may see the instruments whom God has used, and seeing them, and how they were forgiven, may be encouraged for our lesser service. So was it with the Father of the Faithful. He had hours when he was less than his true self. Like all men who have made anything at all, he made mistakes which were entirely lamentable. And it is to one of the worst of these mistakes—his leaving Canaan and going down to Egypt—that I desire to invite your thoughts to-day. First of all, we shall consider what it was that led to this mistake. Secondly, we shall look at the lessons which

Abraham learned from his mistake. Lastly, we shall see how Abraham acted when he was convinced that he had been mistaken.

1. First, then, I want to ask the question, What was it that led Abraham to this action? And to begin with, and on the very surface, there was the new experience of famine. It has often been noted that our worst temptations contain the element of unexpectedness. They come to us by unfamiliar roads, and take us in a moment by surprise. And you may be certain that this time of famine fell with unexpectedness on Abraham. It was an experience that was new to him, and it found him unprepared for the assault. At home in the alluvial wealth of the Euphrates such a thing as famine was unknown. That land was a very garden of the Lord, of an unceasing and prodigal fertility. And it was the very newness of the trial, as of a thing he had never thought or reckoned on, that darkened for a space his trust in God. Was this the land flowing with milk and honey, where he heard the children crying in the night? Was this the goodly land he had been promised, where his flocks were dying by the empty water-courses? It was all dark to Abraham, and all new. He had never reckoned on anything like this. And so for a season it dimmed his trust in

God, and led him to a course that was unworthy.

Again, Abraham was tempted towards Egypt
because others were involved besides himself.
It was not only he who felt the famine ; it was
the women and children who were with him.
Had there only been himself to be considered,
his faith might have been equal to the hour.
He was not the man to fail in his obedience
just because his dinner was in jeopardy.   But
Abraham was very tender-hearted and full of
sympathy for other people ; and the sufferings
of other people tempted him in a way that he
was never tempted by his own.   It was torture
for him to look upon the children and see how
thin and pale they were becoming.   It was
torture for him to look upon the women and
see their sacrifices for the children's sake.   It
was torture for him to look on his old servants,
who had shared in the plenty of his Chaldean
home, and who, as the reward of all their
faithfulness, had scarce a crust to stay their
hunger with.   It has been said that when the
devil strikes at an Englishman he generally
does it through his wife and children.   He
gets at him by the plea of those he loves and
who are dependent on him for their bread.
Are there not many who do unworthy things,
or betake themselves to unworthy callings, or

make the great refusal to be true, because of
the faces that they love so well? That was
the temptation which met Abraham. That
was the perplexity that beset him. He acted
in a way that was unworthy because of those
who were so dear to him. And the strange
thing is that when he acted so, thinking that
he was kindly to his own, he brought his
dearest to the very margin of a womanly
disgrace that is unutterable.

But there was one other reason for his flight
to Egypt which is associated with what is best
in Abraham. There can be little doubt he
travelled southward because it turned his back
on his old home. True, Egypt was a very
fertile land, independent of a precarious rain-
fall. Fed from the secret sources of the Nile,
it was illustrious as a land of plenty. But
over and above that known fertility, with
which, of course, Abraham was familiar, there
was the thought that every step to Egypt took
him further from his native land. It is a mark
of Abraham's greatness that he never repented
of his great decision. He never regretted, in
his hungriest hours, that he had left a land
of plenty at God's call. And if he were tempted
to make for home again, when famine was
laying its gaunt hand upon him, he crushed
that temptation underfoot by marching in the

opposite direction. Every mile he journeyed to the south was another mile 'twixt him and the Euphrates. He was making it harder by every step he took to return to the heathen country of his birth. Knowing the weakness of the human heart and the haunting charm of a forsaken past, deliberately he turned his back upon that past when he struck his tents and made for Egypt. It was a mistake. It was a great mistake. His bounden duty was to have stayed in Canaan. His bounden duty in the land of promise was never to have left the land of promise. And yet was there something noble in his error as there is in the error of a thousand men who, flying from something that is big with danger, rush into the opposite extreme. Extremists are almost invariably wrong. It is generally the middle country which is God's. It is very rarely in a world like this that the truth lies on the extreme limit. Yet who does not feel that there is something noble in every moral recoil that is so passionate, that from the one extreme of a Chaldea it drives a man to the other of an Egypt? The fact is that in many noble lives there is an experience like that of Abraham. It is a parable of the progress of society. It is a picture of the story of the Church. The best does not begin with moderation. It is

with moderation that it ends.   There is Chaldea
first, and Egypt next, and then the sunshine
of the promised land.

2. So far, then, on Abraham's mistake, and
now for some of the lessons which he learned
from it.   One of the first lessons he was taught
was this : it was the insufficiency of cleverness.

There is one thing you may notice here.   It
is an omission that is worth regarding.   There
is not a sign that Abraham cried to God about
the wisdom of going down to Egypt.   He may
have spoken about it when he prayed, as when
we pray we touch on many things.   But that
he went to God and begged Him for guidance,
of that there is not a trace in Scripture.   The
whole impression left on us is this, that Abraham acted on his own initiative, that he felt
himself perfectly competent and capable to
take the management of the whole matter.   It
is told of a celebrated English statesman that
he regarded himself as capable of anything.
If he had been ordered to command the fleet
he would have done it without a moment's
hesitancy.   And one cannot wonder if there
were times when Abraham was liable to be
tempted just like that, he was so masterful,
he was so apt to rule, he was so brave and
ready in emergencies.   It was a very clever
bit of policy to try to pass off Sarah as his

sister. On the surface of it that was not a
lie, for Sarah was Abraham's half-sister. But
it was far too clever to be wise, and it was far
too clever to be good, and the incident just
reveals the spirit in which Abraham managed
this Egyptian business. He fell back upon his
own astuteness. He thought that all would be
well if he were shrewd. He thought that all
that was needed for success was a cool brain
and a politic behaviour. And then God laid
him in the very dust and shamed him in the
presence of the heathen, and showed him what
a mistake he had committed in imagining that
he was self-sufficient. It is told of the great
astronomer Laplace that he presented his work
on astronomy to Napoleon. Napoleon read
it and admired it greatly, but asked the author
why God was never named in it. ' Sire,' was
Laplace's answer to the Emperor, ' I had no
need of that hypothesis.' Are there not multitudes whose daily life is like the answer of
that French astronomer ? Are there not many
so confident of self that they think they have
no need of that hypothesis ? And that is one
spiritual worth of these mistakes into which
our very abilities may lead us, that they help
us to feel our utter need of God and of a wisdom
higher than our own.

Another lesson which Abraham learned was

this. It was the loving watchfulness of God. He came back from Egypt with a deepened sense of the care of the shepherd for his wandering sheep. You must remember that till this hour of failure Abraham had been splendidly obedient. He had obeyed the call and left his home. He had never swerved from his appointed path. What Abraham had learned up to this hour is how God blesses the man who is obedient. He had never experienced yet the love of heaven to the man who has wandered from the heavenly way. It was that discovery he made in Egypt. It was the mercy of heaven to the wanderer. It was the love that would not let him go, though he had strayed away from his appointed place. And I have often thought that Christ had this in view when He looked back across the gulf of years and said, ' Your father Abraham rejoiced to see My day: and he saw it, and was glad.' It was then that Abraham saw, as in a vision, the shepherd going forth to seek his sheep. It was then that he saw the father of the prodigal and how he loved his son in the far country. It was then that he who had been always righteous, but now was fallen upon a day of failure, heard as it were the voice from heaven which said, ' I came not to call the righteous but sinners to repentance.'

But there is one thing more that Abraham learned. It was a bitter and salutary lesson. He learned the shame a good man always feels when he is convicted by the world. Who the Pharaoh was who is here mentioned it will never perhaps be possible to say. It does not really matter who he was. The important thing is to notice what he was. And judging him by the standards of his time, when so much was lawful that is forbidden now, we may say that he was a very noble character who acted in a very noble way. It is he who is the great man of the story. It is he who is generous and kingly-hearted. It is he who, finding he had been tricked by Abraham, deals with Abraham in such a lofty way. And you can picture the shame in Abraham's heart when he, the child of vision and of covenant, had to confess that in the point of character he was beaten by a heathen prince. It is always a sad thing when that occurs, and it occurs even to this hour. There are men who will tell you that when they needed help the world was kinder to them than the Church. There are men who will tell you that in their hour of trial, when they needed generous and kindly treatment, the hand that grasped them and the heart that cheered them was that of some one who made no profession. It is a pity that

such things should be. It is more than a
pity, it is shameful. It is a humbling and a
sorry thing when a Pharaoh can rebuke an
Abraham. All which should make us doubly
earnest to make our calling and election sure,
and to keep ourselves by prayer and pains in
the love of the Lord Jesus Christ.

3. In closing, let me direct your thoughts
to the conduct of Abraham after his mistake.
How did he act ? What course did he pursue
when he discovered that he had been mistaken?
So much depends upon that in every life that it
is a matter of the highest moment. All of us
make lamentable errors ; how do we act when
we discover them ? That is the question we
must ask of Abraham, and that is the question
to which there is an answer.

The point to note is that when he saw his
error, Abraham in the truest way acknowledged it. He made his confession like the
prodigal son, by going back again to his own
place. But perhaps you say, 'Was he not
driven back ? Did not Pharaoh send him away
and make him go ? And if he was forced to
march by armed men, can that be regarded
as a mark of penitence ? ' If you will take the
thirteenth chapter and look at the opening
verses, you will see at once there is more in it
than that. It is true that Abraham was forced

from Egypt. It is true he was escorted to the frontier. But then, what did he do when he got there, and stood in Canaan a free man again? The Bible tells us he went back to Bethel to the place where his tent had been pitched at the beginning, back to the site of his first altar, and there he called upon the name of the Lord. He might have called upon the Lord in other places. Deliberately he chose that early scene. He wanted to get right back to that sweet spot where once he had been obedient and had trusted. He wanted to resume his life again from the point where he had turned away from God, and that action was his true confession.

There are few things more indicative of strength of character than a readiness to acknowledge that one has been mistaken, few things that augur better for success than the open eye for possible mistake. The artist may yield to some prevailing fashion that robs his pictures of their charm and delicacy. The writer may fall for a season under influences that take the strength and music from his style. The business man may be led to give his energies to something that he had better not have touched. The minister may countenance innovations which do not benefit worship but retard it. Now, it is never an easy

task and never a pleasant one just to acknowledge that one has been mistaken. For some
natures it is incredibly hard, there is such
stubbornness and pride to combat. And it is
when a man is brought into such hours and
when his pride is fighting with his wisdom,
that he should seek the company of Abraham
and remember what it was that made him
great. He went right back again to his first
altar. He went before the eyes of all his
clan. He was too big a soul to think he was
infallible. He was too wise to prolongate his
errors. So by his errors no less than by his
achievements, by his mistakes as well as by
his victories, did he build up a life that at
the last had the 'Well done, thou good and
faithful servant.'

ABRAHAM, on his return from Egypt, was a
great deal wealthier than when he entered it.
Lot also had shared in his prosperity, and was
now a man of independent wealth. There was
a forest of tents where they encamped ; there
was the lowing of unnumbered cattle ; there
was all the mingled excitement and confusion
of a great multitude of men and beasts ; until
at last this evident prosperity became, as it
often does, the cause of trouble, and led to
very unexpected consequences. The quarrelling began among the servants. They were
overworked, and had too little sleep, and with
the strain of it their nerves were all on edge.
And so when they drove to pasture in the
morning and found that some one else was
there before them, you may be certain there
would be angry words. From angry words it
is not far to blows, and the blows came speedily
and surely. It was a most unedifying spectacle
in the household of professing saints. And
what made it more unedifying still was that
the Canaanite and the Perizzite were in the

land, eager, if I know human nature, to have some handle against godly Abraham. That is why quarrelling in covenant circles is always so bitterly to be deplored. The Canaanite and the Perizzite are with us still, though Abraham has gone to his home. And they are as watchful to find fault to-day and as delighted with every angry voice as they were when they watched with a malicious joy this quarrelling of the shepherds of the Lord. It was then that Abraham took instant action. He saw that Lot and he must separate. He knew that the kitchen quarrel of to-day might be the drawing-room quarrel of to-morrow. And so he led out Lot on to the uplands and showed him the kingdom and all the glory of it and bade him choose whatever he desired.

Now there are two things to be noted in this difference ; and the first is that wealth was at the back of it. Had Abraham and Lot not been so prosperous, the trouble would never have arisen. There are many who think if they were only prosperous their troubles would be gone, and gone for ever. Could they only come back from Egypt with a fortune, the land of promise would be a land of peace. But all that Abraham had to suffer when he was struggling across the barren desert was not so bitter to his generous heart as the

kind of thing he had to suffer now. Then Lot
and he had been the best of friends. There
had been no barrier in their intercourse.
Bound in kinship by the ties of blood, they
had together worshipped at the altar. But
now there was estrangement 'twixt the two,
with the bitter necessity of separation, and the
whole trouble sprang from their prosperity.
There are few things sadder in society than
just that separating power of wealth. How
often does it put relatives at variance and
move them quite apart from one another.
How often it makes them suspicious of each
other and mars the liberty of social intercourse, giving to every word and every deed
a certain aspect of calculation. The other
feature to be noted here is how generously
Abraham waived his rights. He treated Lot
as if he were his equal, and Lot was very far
from being his equal. Abraham was the elder
of the two. His was the right to choose by
seniority. He was the leader of the pilgrimage ; and more, he had been as a father to
his nephew. Yet when separation was inevitable and a division of the land was necessary,
Abraham urged nothing of all that. He might
have said, and said with perfect justice, ' It
is for me to take what I desire.' He might
have settled the whole matter by himself, in-

different to Lot's pleasure or displeasure. And there must have been something generous in the man, something kingly-hearted and magnanimous, when he took his nephew and showed him all the land and told him to choose any part he pleased. There are men who might have acted so by nature in a spirit of uncalculating recklessness. There are men like Esau who throw away their birthright, because they have never realised its value. But Abraham acted in another spirit and with the clearest sense of what he offered. His generosity to Lot sprang from another and a deeper root. It sprang from his deep sense that God was his, that his true possession was in God. It sprang from his belief that all he needed was his, and his for ever, in the promise. It was that which made him incapable of selfishness and willing that others should have ample room, and certain that no human choice could take from him what was divinely pledged. There is always that magnanimity in faith when faith is active in the human heart. It is not careful about being robbed, for it knows that none can rob it of its own. It is willing to take the lowest room ; will not grudge the choice to other people ; has learned what this means which was said by Jesus, ' It is more blessed to give than to receive.'

So treated then by Abraham, Lot chose, as we all know, the land of Sodom. It was a choice which had disastrous consequences. Now every choice that a man makes reveals him. It shows something of his secret heart. It opens a lattice on his real nature, which is so often hidden by appearances. And I want to ask, What do we learn of Lot as we see him making this momentous choice? What does this choice tell us of the man?

In the first place, we cannot fail to see how destitute he was of finer feelings. The very fact that he agreed to choose shows that something was wanting in the man. Had there been a spark of gratitude in Lot, he never would have accepted Abraham's offer. He would have seen it to be utterly unfitting that he, the younger man, should be the arbiter. He would have recognised his uncle's chivalry, of a piece with all his previous bearing, and recognising it, would have refused to trade on it to his own advantage. It is characteristic of the man that he made no move in that direction. He seems to have been dead to filial feeling, insensible to the claims of gratitude. Evidently he had a shallow heart which was of little use in an emergency, and was incapable of such warmth of feeling as might have led him to his proper course. Brethren, there are times when one's best guide is just the generous instinct of the heart. There are times when men, confronted by alternatives, do well to listen to their deepest feelings. There are times when self-interest has its opportunity and a way seems to be open for advancement, yet when all that is deepest and divinest in us rises in rebellion at that way. Woe to the man who, in an hour like that, crushes the quiet promptings of his heart. There may be more of God in a dim instinct than in a hundred reasons and excuses. Let a man throw himself upon these secret movings which he can never explain and never analyse, and often when confronted by alternatives he will be spared the misery of Lot.

Again, we discover from the choice that Lot was essentially unspiritual. It is often our choices that betray that. It was his choice that made it plain in Lot. What is the mark of a spiritual man? what is really meant by spirituality? Is a man spiritual just because he prays, or comes to the sanctuary, or reads his Bible? It goes deeper than all that. A man is spiritual when the things of the spirit are the great realities for him. A man is spiritual who lives and moves under the felt power of the unseen. A man is spiritual to whom the things of sense are but the shadows of things that are invisible, and who in every choice that he is called to immediately takes account of the unseen. The carnal man judges by the senses. The spiritual man judges by the spirit. The carnal looks at temporal advantage, the spiritual at the welfare of the soul. The carnal thinks first of his own interest, and how that interest may be advanced, but the spiritual seeks first the Kingdom of God. Far oftener than in speech it is in choices we show we are unspiritual. If the invisible were real to us, how often you and I had chosen differently. And Lot reveals himself as an unspiritual man, spite of all his fellowship with Abraham, when he looks eastward and sees the land of Sodom and chooses it on the verdict of his eye.

But I think this choice shows even more than that. I think it shows how Lot was hankering backward. I think it shows how Lot, since he left home, had dragged at each remove a lengthening chain. Mark you, as he looked eastward, what he saw. He saw a land of tropical fertility. He saw a land that reminded him of home, a veritable garden of the Lord. And he knew also that there were cities there, with the settled comforts of a city life, the same as he had known in Babylonia. Lot was a little wearied of his tent. He was

wearied of this wandering existence. He had
never been really whole-hearted, though he
had often thought he was, in Abraham's company. And now perhaps he was less so than
ever, for he was fresh from sojourning in
Egypt, and in Egypt he had enjoyed again
all the comfort of a city life. The fact is that
Lot, although a pilgrim, had never really
broken with his past. It was the faith of
Abraham that had moved him rather than a
faith that was his own. And that is what is
made apparent now, when he leaves Abraham
and chooses Sodom. The man is hankering
to enjoy again the life he had forsaken long
ago. How often do professing Christians betray
themselves in such a way as that ! How often
by their choices they declare that they are a
little weary of the tent ! They do it by the way
in which they dwell on the things that happened in their day of liberty. They do it by
the ambitions which they cherish, and cherish
perhaps in secret, for their children. They do
it by the choice of what is easy, by leaving the
stern uplands for the valley, by seizing the
opportunity to get away from Abraham and
live again in the fellowship of Sodom. Sooner
or later a man is self-revealed if he has not
the root of the matter in him. Sooner or later
comes the decisive hour when God discovers

what is in his heart. It takes more than fellow-ship with lofty souls to carry us to the kingdom and the crown. It takes the living fellowship of God experienced and tested every day.

Notable once more is this, as we regard this choice of long ago. It is how slowly and how gradually the consequences of it showed themselves. When Lot left Abraham he took his tent with him. He still intended to use it as his home. Somewhere in the valley he would pitch it where he might still have privacy and peace. But when a man pitches his tent toward Sodom, he always goes further than he meant to go. The heart that is hankering for the town to-day will be entering the city gates to-morrow. Had you told Lot when he said farewell to Abraham that soon he would be a citizen of Sodom, how all that was best in him would have denied it, and denied it with evident sincerity. Yet by and by Lot had his home in Sodom, and he was busy trading in its streets, and, worst of all, he saw his daughters married to citizens of that disgusting city. It is often the children who have to pay the penalty for the foolish conduct of the fathers. It is they who have to suffer and be miserable because their fathers have forgotten God. And I think that the misery of Lot was full when he went to visit his daughters in their homes, and thought how he, by tampering with his conscience, had brought them to this nameless infamy. That is the worst of every choice that a man makes against his better nature. Not all at once does it reveal its perils. Not in one life does it exhaust itself. It hurls its curse upon the helpless family and visits with misery the sons and daughters, until God in providence puts out His hand and the family ceases to exist.

In closing, let us return to Abraham after Lot was separated from him. Left alone in a strange land, he is a pathetic and solitary figure. He had loved his nephew in spite of his nephew's shallowness. He had prayed for him, I doubt not, every day. He had wrestled with God for him, and hoped the best, and borne with him, as a father with his son. And now that he was gone Abraham was lonely, and there was something lacking in his life, and he lay sleepless in his tent of nights, and thought of the wanderer who was away. There are men of iron who can pass through life and be but little affected by its changes. Abraham was not a man of iron. He had a deep and loving and sympathetic heart. And though he had too much of Hebrew pride ever to wear his heart upon his sleeve, we can believe how sore it was in secret. Then, too,

the fear would visit him sometimes lest he had
been mistaken in his action. He would hear
the murmuring among his servants that the
best pasturage had gone to Lot. Until at last
Abraham grew despondent, and everything
was mysterious and dark, and sometimes he
may have been tempted to believe that his
way was passed over from his God. It was
then, mark you, that God spoke to Abraham.
It was then He came to him with glorious
promise. He bade him rise and survey all
the land, and told him it would be his for
ever. He came to him when everything was
darkest, and when the heart of Abraham was
sad, and cheered him with such a word of
hope as brought the singing of the birds again.

Brethren, among all our times of peril, and
such times are not few in any pilgrimage, there
are not many which are quite so perilous as
our recurrent seasons of reaction. When we
have taken up our cross in silence, when we
have bravely faced unwelcome duty, might we
not hope that in the following hours all the
heaven would be blue above us? Yet how
often that is not the case, how often we are
despondent and dispirited, how often everything seems to go against us when we have
striven to be quietly true. Now test what I
am going to say by your own hearts. Test it

by your own experience. Is it not often in such a time of shadow that God becomes most real? We learn that there is a love that we can lean on. We learn there is a promise we can trust. We learn that stooping there is peace for us which the world cannot give and cannot take away. 'And the Lord said unto Abraham, after that Lot was separated from him.' The Lord was waiting for that separation that He might speak His richest and His best. And so I take it, He is waiting still till some of us surrender what is sweet, that He may reveal Himself to us in another way than He does unto the world.

WHEN Abraham was returning from his rescue of Lot, two very notable incidents occurred. The one was his meeting with the king of Sodom, and the other his meeting with Melchizedek. Rejoiced at being rid of his oppressor, the king of Sodom was in a grateful mood. Let Abraham but give him back his prisoners, and he might keep all the booty to himself. But that is just what Abraham would not do. Not a thread, not a shoe-latchet, would he accept at the king of Sodom's hands. Never would he have it said of him that he owed his fortune to the king of Sodom. Abraham had heard within his heart that question that was asked by Christ after long ages, ' What shall it profit a man if he gain the whole world and lose his own soul ? '

But prior to this there was another meeting, even more remarkable than that. It was the meeting of Abraham and Melchizedek. As Abraham was on his homeward road he saw a figure coming down the valley. There were tokens of royalty about the visitors. There was a retinue of servants bearing food. It was Melchizedek, king of Salem, the priest of the most high God, and he had come to give Abraham his blessing. Out of the shadow quietly he comes. For a single instant he is in the light. And Abraham bows to him as to a greater, and pays him tithes and gets his benediction. And then the cloud comes driving down the valley and wraps this strange figure in its folds, and we are alone with Abraham again.

This Melchizedek is one of the most mysterious characters in Scripture. He is like the bird in the old Saxon apologue that flits in a moment across the lighted hall. He was some one of incomparable greatness, for Abraham, the friend of God, was less than he. Flushed with his triumph over the king of Elam, Abraham none the less is at his feet. Yet who he was, or of what race he came, or by what title he made Abraham bow, of that we know absolutely nothing. Still more strange, and deepening the mystery, Melchizedek was a priest of the true God. He lived in a country of the vilest heathenism where the name of God had never been declared. Yet somehow he had come to know that name, and somehow he had been endued with priesthood, and that with a warrant of such convincing power that

Abraham, meeting him, gave him tithes of all. Strange figure, emerging from the darkness, clothed in royalty and priestly grace. Whence came he? Where had he been cradled? What was the mother who bore him on her bosom? On all that the Word of God is silent. He had no father or beginning of days. Of all the patriarchs there are genealogies; of Melchizedek there is none.

Now you cannot wonder that on this mysterious figure the thought of Israel should have brooded much. They felt there was more in it than met the ear. Reverencing Abraham as they did, regarding him as the faithful, every life that came in touch with his was enshrined in the memory of Israel. And when among such lives they met with one whose place with God was higher than the patriarch's, it moved them with a certain awe. They felt that its significance for them was not exhausted by that single incident. They felt that there was something in that meeting that it would take the future to explain. So gradually as there rose before them the vision of a Christ who was to come, that vision blended with Melchizedek. They did not think Melchizedek was Christ. That is the fancy of a later day. They did not think that it was Christ Himself who stepped out of the shadow of the vale.

But as they meditated on Melchizedek, and how deeply they meditated none can tell, more and more God made it plain to them that the Christ who was to come would be like that. It was to that thought that the Psalmist gave expression in the 110th Psalm. He has caught a vision of the coming Lord, and he cries, ' Thou art a priest for ever after the order of Melchizedek.' It is that thought that is amplified in Hebrews with a fulness and insight that are wonderful, or rather let me say that would be wonderful if we did not see in it the Holy Spirit. Come, then, and let us try this morning to see why Melchizedek suggested Christ. What was it in that mysterious figure that seemed to cast a light on the Messiah ? There are two or three points we shall consider.

1. In the first place, Melchizedek stood alone. He is a solitary and unconnected figure. He was the priest of the true and living God, and yet his ancestry is all unknown. Now it is difficult for you and me to realise how that impressed a Jew. To us the Levitical priesthood is a name ; to them it was the mightiest of realities. And the one essential in the Jewish priesthood—rather, let me say, the first essential—was that the priest should be a member of a certain family. No man could be a priest

among the Jews unless he were certain of his genealogy. He must have the right descent upon his mother's side. Without that he might have every gift that would qualify for the discharge of priesthood, yet never could he be a priest of Aaron's order. Now, brethren, do you not see at once how different it was with Melchizedek. All the scribes and Pharisees together could never discover who his father was. He had no father, says the writer to the Hebrews. He means that God kept his fatherhood a secret. God showed how little He recked of genealogies by throwing him thus into the Scripture story. Melchizedek was not a link in a long chain. He was not one of an unbroken series. He stood alone, a priest in his own person, and thus he suggested the Lord Jesus Christ. Many attempts have been made to account for Jesus Christ by His environment. And never perhaps were such attempts so thorough as they are with a certain critical school to-day. Every influence that could have played upon Him, every vision that could have stirred His boyhood, is offered to us in the name of scholarship, as helping to account for Jesus Christ. Shall I tell you what the result has been? The result has been very unexpected. It has been to impress upon all reverent hearts the incommunicable glory of the Lord. It has been to show us that He stands alone, uplifted above every human sequence, as separate from the before and after as this mysterious figure of the vale. Christ is not one link in a long chain. He is not an item of a long succession. He did not receive his priesthood from another, and not to another did He hand it on. His is a priesthood of the personality, inherent in Himself and His for ever. He is a priest after the order of Melchizedek.

2. Again, Melchizedek suggested Christ because of his incomparable greatness. Not only was he a lonely figure. He was a figure of surpassing grandeur. These solitary men are often so, these men who haunt the shadow and the silence. We are always ready to invest with grandeur mysterious and inexplicable figures. But remember it was not on that account that the Jew was awestruck at Melchizedek. It was because of what happened at this interview. You must remember that in Jewish eyes Abraham was the greatest man who ever lived. He held a place peerless and unparalleled in the reverence of the Jewish people. Not Moses on the heights of Sinai, not Solomon in all his glory, were so exalted in the Jewish heart as the old patriarch from Ur. Moses was the man of God ; but Abraham was the friend

of God. ' We are the children of Abraham,'
they cried. It was the proudest title they could
bear. And all their hopes of blessedness in
paradise when at last they should awake and
should be satisfied, were centred on the happy
prospect that they should be for ever upon
Abraham's bosom. Now think of it ! Here
was a meeting between Father Abraham and
some one else. It occurred in an hour when
Abraham was transfigured, for he had fought
with kings and been victorious. Yet even in
that hour Abraham bows, and gets a blessing
from some one greater, and offers tithes to him
as to a person who was more representative of
God than he, closer to God even than His
friend, mightier than the father of the faithful !
Can you wonder that this mysterious figure
should have come to speak to men of Jesus
Christ ! It was that grandeur which was
before the Psalmist ; it was that which touched
the writer to the Hebrews, when with a vision
full of Christ they cried, ' Thou art a priest
after the order of Melchizedek.'

3. But again Melchizedek suggested Christ
because he was a king as well as priest. In his
person he united the two offices, the office of
kingship and of priesthood. He was a king.
He was the king of Salem. He had the power
and the rank of royalty. But not only was he

the king of Salem ; he was also priest of the Most High God. And the more men meditated on that union, that blending in the one person of two offices, the more they found in this mysterious visitant a dim foreshadowing of the Messiah. I do not think that I should err were I to say this about the history of Israel. Perhaps the saddest thing in that sad story is the separation of the priest and king. Had priest and king only been at one, what a different story Israel would have had ! Had they but leaned upon each other's strength, that little nation had been irresistible. For then the power in the hands of kingship would have moved in union with the will of God, and the blessing of God, which was the priest's to mediate, would have rested upon the power of the king. It was the severance of king and priest that lay at the very heart of Israel's tragedy. Ever suspicious of each other's office, nothing was possible save wreckage. And so it was that when prophetic souls looked forward through the darkness to Messiah, they felt, and it was God who made them feel, that He would be priest and king in His own person. So looking forward they looked backward too, and lo, the thing that was to be had been. Here in Melchizedek there was a king, and yet he was a priest of the true God. So always in their vision of the Coming One there mingled thoughts of this mysterious figure, until the Psalmist cried in his great song, ' Thou art a priest after the order of Melchizedek.' When John, a prisoner in Patmos, had his vision of Christ, do you remember what it was he saw ? He saw one who like a sceptre held seven stars, and he knew that he was looking on a king. But the figure was also clothed in a long garment, and girt with a golden girdle on the breast, and robe and girdle were not kingly dress—they were the official robings of the priest. He knew, although he does not put it so, that Christ was of the order of Melchizedek. He saw that day the sceptre of the king, he saw the robe and girdle of the priest. And that is always the vision that we need, the vision that is mighty to redeem, the vision that has come with priestly pardon and sealed it with the grace of kingly power. It is not enough that Christ should be a king, for we are rebels and we need forgiveness. It is not enough that Christ should be a priest, for we are very weak and we need power. But Christ is both. He is our priest and king. He pardons and He empowers the faint. He is a priest for ever, God be praised, after the order of Melchizedek.

4. Once more there was a suggestion of the

Coming One in the name of the mysterious
visitor. He was Melchizedek, king of Salem,
and the name he bore was big with meaning.
We must remember that in the East names
meant a great deal more than they do to us.
To us there is nothing important in a name.
We value it only for its associations. To us
a name is but a badge, a title to distinguish
individuals, a handy and swift means of
recognition. But it was very different in the
East, remember. A name there was a mysterious thing. It had within it a prophecy
of character. It hinted at its bearer's destiny.
Just as the name of God, as says the Catechism,
is that whereby He is made known to us, so
in the name of every man and woman there
was some revelation of the heart. You ask,
perhaps, how that is possible when it is the
parents who bestow the name ? You ask how
a name could be significant when it is given
to a little child ? The answer is that to a Jew
God was always busy in such choices, leading
the parents, though they never knew it, to a
name that would be fitting for the character.
So closely identified were character and name,
that when the one was changed so was the
other. Jacob becomes Israel, Saul becomes
Paul, Simon in the hands of Jesus becomes
Peter. And when the last great change shall

come to us, and we shall awake in glory and be satisfied, not only will there be a new song there, but there will also be a new name.

Filled then with thoughts like that about the mystic significance of names, prophet and psalmist found a world of meaning in the name given to this lonely figure. He was Melchizedek, and what does that mean? Melchizedek means the king of righteousness. He was a good man, he was a righteous man, he walked with a perfect heart before his God. And then the city that he ruled was Salem, and Salem is the Hebrew word for peace. Peace like a river flowed in all its streets, and flowed there because the king was righteous. That was the picture in the heart of Israel as they brooded and brooded deep upon Melchizedek.

They saw a city where was perfect peace because on its throne there was a perfect king. No sound of war was heard within its gates. No trumpet call disturbed the vineyard dresser. It was a place of happiness and rest under Melchizedek, the king of righteousness. Can you wonder that when Christ appeared that ancient picture should have been revived? Can you wonder that looking at Jesus and His kingdom, men thought of that ancient city in the vale? The greatest gift of Jesus Christ was peace : peace with God, peace in heart and conscience. It was of peace the herald-angels sang, and the last legacy of Christ was peace. And this deep peace, what is at its source ? It is the perfect righteousness of Christ. It is His obedience even to the Cross that you and I might be reconciled to God. Thrilling with the gladness of that news, men hailed the kingdom as the Salem mystical. Looking to Jesus in His perfect goodness, they cried, ' Here is Melchizedek indeed.' All they had pictured had come true at last. It was incarnate in the Lord Jesus Christ. He was their King, He was their Priest for ever after the order of Melchizedek.

SOME thirteen years had passed away since the hour when Ishmael had been born, and in all these years there is no trace that God had revealed Himself to Abraham. No disaster had befallen Abraham. No plague had visited his sheep or cattle. His life had outwardly been very prosperous, and as rich in peace as in prosperity. Yet all the time the heavens had been as brass, no voice from the beyond had spoken to him, no vision had ever broken on his sleep as he lay amid the silent hills at Mamre. Is it not thus that men are often punished when they fall away from obedience to God? Outwardly everything is just the same as in the day when trust was lively and sincere, but inwardly there is a dryness of the spirit, a loss of joy in all religious exercises, an absence both in service and in prayer of the inward witness of the Holy Ghost. Brethren, God serves many purposes by what we know as spiritual desertion. There are times when He hides His face from us in love as He hid it from Jesus on the Cross. But I pray you remember that that inward deadness, that absence of inward joy and peace, may be with us just as it was with Abraham, the penalty we pay for disobedience.

Notable too is Abraham's frame of mind when God renewed His covenant again. It is so different from what we should have looked for in the hour that told of the crowning of his hopes. Abraham was now an aged man, and the one promise was yet unfulfilled. The child of the covenant had not been born, though promised to him many a year ago. But now at last the joyful hour was come, and God drew near with the annunciation, and all that Abraham had waited for so long was to be his at last and his immediately. Surely within the old man's heart there will be nothing but a tide of joy. Surely he will sing as Mary sang, ' My soul doth magnify the Lord.' Ah, sirs ! we might have looked for that ; but that was not what burst from Abraham's heart. ' O that Ishmael might live before Thee ! ' was the one thought that rose on to his tongue.

Now I want you to think for a moment what that means. I want you rather to think what it betrays. You know who Ishmael was ; who his mother was. Ishmael was now a lad of fourteen years. He was the only child

within that tent. Probably he was a fine
handsome boy, dark-skinned and graceful like
his Egyptian mother. And he was full of
spirit and of courage, and the light of the open
world was in his eyes, and every one loved him
for his handsome form and for his merriment
and for his recklessness. Can you wonder
that that attractive youth had entwined himself about the old man's heart? Can you
wonder that Abraham, always a little lonely,
had come to love him more deeply than he
knew? Can you wonder that when the
moment came when God revealed to him the
birth of Isaac, his deepest feeling was a pang
for Ishmael? 'O that Ishmael might live
before Thee!' He was not glad as he once
thought to be. He did not worship in ador-
ing gratitude. His heart was filled already
with a child whose birth had been a disobedience. So when at last after those weary
years the moment came that was to crown
his life, the glory of it all was dimmed for
Abraham, and dimmed just because Ishmael
was there.

My brother, is it not often so? Must we not
watch lest it be so with us? It is one of the
penalties we always pay when we anticipate
the ways of God. It is a sad thing when we
never win that which we may have waited for

for years. It is far sadder when we win it and find it has lost its power to make us glad. And nine times out of ten when that is so, it means that in the weary years of waiting we have been tampering with faith in God and seeking the satisfactions of the flesh. When a man grasps with carnal hands to-day what God intended him to have to-morrow, God does not always keep from him to-morrow the blessing that was treasured for that hour. Sometimes He gives it, gives it in its fulness, but oh, the penalty we pay is this—that all its charm is gone, and all its mystery, and it has lost its power to make us glad. Young men and women, keep yourselves pure. Do not anticipate where God delays. Do not destroy the glory of the future by conduct that is disobedience to the best. It is a sorry thing when all is given at last that heaven in its bounty can bestow, and the only answer in the heart is this, ' O that Ishmael might live before Thee ! '

It seems to have been very shortly afterwards that Abraham had this visit of the angels, and with one exception there is no scene in his life that is more familiar to us than that visit. It was the hour of noon. The day was sultry. There was a haze of heat upon the downs. The birds were silent in the forest trees. The cattle were standing idly in the water. All work had ceased, the heat was so intense ; there wasn't a figure moving on the fields, and Abraham, under the shadow of his oak tree, was sitting dreamily in the tent-door. It was then he lifted up his eyes, and lo ! three strangers were approaching. Unprotected from the pitiless sun, they were clearly making for the tent. Whereon Abraham, with that noble hospitality which has ever been one of the virtues of the East, ran to meet them and bowed himself before them, and made them lords of everything he had. It was not an uncommon thing to happen then. It is not an uncommon thing to happen now. Read any book of travels in the East, and you will light on such receptions still. But for Abraham it was the day of days—these three might be dusty, but they were divine ; and at the great day the Lord will say to Abraham, ' I was a stranger, and ye took Me in.'

Now there are two things in that visit we must note, and the first is, what was the purpose of it ? Why was it that now and now alone God spoke to Abraham in such a guise ? Hitherto God had often spoken to him. In the future He was to speak again. And sometimes it was in visions of the night and sometimes by the quiet voice within. Why, then, on this occasion only did God depart from His accustomed dealing? I think the reason is not hard to find.

There is a beautiful picture in the Doré Bible in illustration of this hour at Mamre. You see the patriarch seated at his tent. You feel the sultriness of noonday heat. But what of the visitors who are approaching? Doré has furnished them with angel wings. They are radiant creatures of a brighter world, glowing with the light that lives in heaven. And it is there that Doré has gone wrong. He has forgotten the writer to the Hebrews. It was not in the garb of angels that they came. It was in the guise of ordinary men. There was nothing to declare they were exceptional, nothing to tell that they were come from heaven. Weary and travel-stained and parched with thirst, they came to Abraham as common travellers. And *that* was the essence of the hour, that was the very purpose of the visit—it was God discovering the heart of Abraham. And Abraham never dreamed that God was there. Hitherto, mark you, whenever God had spoken Abraham had recognised the speaker. There was no mistaking it. It was the voice of God. And Abraham had bowed in lowly reverence. But now there was no hint of the divine, no token of the glory at the gate, and the question was, how would the man behave in that unconscious nearness of his Lord. I need not tell you how he stood the test. He stood the test of the ordinary hour. Had they been angels such as Doré pictured, he couldn't have given them a nobler welcome. And I need not tell you that when these same angels went down to Sodom for a like discovery they were treated with the indignities of hell.

Brethren, in your life and mine there have been hours when we knew perfectly who was speaking to us. We were sure of this, if we were sure of anything, that the voice that spoke to us was that of God. It may have been in the hour of bereavement when everything lay shattered at our feet ; it may have been in the hour of decision when we had been praying for light upon the path ; it may have been when we had greatly sinned and had been sorely punished for our sin ; and then we heard, clear as a silver bell, ' Though your sins be as scarlet, they shall be as white as snow.' In such hours we hear the voice of God. We know that God is very near to us. Sooner would we doubt our hands and feet than doubt the stooping love of the Almighty. But remember that for one hour like that, when God is unmistakable and evident,

there are a thousand hours in every life when
He is present and He is not known. He
comes to us just as He came to Abraham,
wrapped in the garment of the common
traveller. He comes in the duty of the
common day, in the opportunity of common
hours. He comes in the lights and shadows
of the home, in the petty battles we must fight
with self, in the unheroic crosses we must carry,
and carry oftentimes with little sympathy.
It is such hours that are the sorest test. It is
of such hours that life is built. Life is not
raised above the stormy waters like some
new island by the shock of earthquake. Life
is built, as is the coral island, by infinitesimal
toiling in the deeps, till it is raised into a thing
of beauty where beyond the breakers there is
peace.

Then the other notable feature of this visit
is this. It is the mingled nature of the message. It is the blending of sunshine and of
storm in the message which the angels brought.
I don't know how that may appear to others,
but to me it is peculiarly impressive. To me
it is one of those unconscious arguments that
witness the heavenly origin of Scripture. It
is so unlike what man would have devised ;
so alien from *our* carrying of tidings. It is so
consonant with all we know of God, and of

His revelation to the human race. Think of it! these angels came with joy. They were the herald-angels of the promise. They came to make the heart of Sarah joyful with the great news of the child who was to be. And yet the very voice that spoke of that, spoke of the curse that was to fall on Sodom, passed from the radiance as of a summer morning into the pitchy blackness of the night. It is not thus we send abroad our tidings. We keep the sorrow separate from the joy. We say, ' Now this shall be a day of happiness, and not a shadow must be suffered on it.' But I think you will always find that when God speaks, when He reveals Himself to human hearts, the sorrow and the joy are strangely mingled as in the message of a single voice. Is it not so with His good gift of children ? How happy the children make us, and how sorrowful. Is it not so with the good gift of love ? What a paradise it is, and what a pain. Was it not so with the gift of Jesus Christ, who was a Man of sorrows and ac-quainted with grief, and yet, in the very heart of all His sorrow, spoke in ecstasy about His joy ? It is that voice of all the ages that I hear speaking in the tent at Mamre. It blends the gladness and the gloom together in a way that was finally perfected in Christ. It makes the heart of Sarah like a song in the good news that she was waiting for ; and then in that same conversation it draws the curtain from the mouth of hell.

Students of Genesis have written much on God's revealing to Abraham the doom of Sodom. They have discussed at length what was the reason of it. We know why the birth of Isaac was foretold. It lay inside the covenant of grace. It was the crowning of the gracious purpose that had been guiding Abraham from the first. But Sodom lay outside the covenant ; it was outwith the circuit of the promise, and men have wondered why, to Abraham, God revealed the story of its fall.

Well, there are certain reasons on the surface that help us to explain that difficulty. For instance, Abraham was the friend of God, and this confidence was a token of that friendship. Then again, it had been promised Abraham that all the nations were to be blessed in him. All the nations—and Sodom was a nation, and he was hoping that Sodom would be blessed. And so God told him what was going to happen, lest happening without a word of warning it might have made him stagger through unbelief. It was partly for these reasons that God acted. These two are written in the chapter here. But there is another reason hidden in the very marrow of the chapter. And I want to try to make it plain to you, for it is the most important of them all.

Now think of it. When the news of Sodom was vouchsafed to Abraham he had just learned the greatest lesson of his life. He had been taught in the great news of Isaac that the just shall live by faith. He had tried to work out his own salvation, and Ishmael was the result of that. He had schemed and striven to force the promise on, and all his scheming had been ineffectual. Through hope deferred, through plannings baffled, through purposes scattered to the winds of heaven, he had been taught that not the labours of his hands could fulfil Thy laws demands. ' By grace, ye are saved through faith, not of yourselves ; not of works, lest any man should boast.' It was that glorious truth that broke on Abraham when, in his impotence, he heard of Isaac. And it was then, then in that very hour when he was taught the sovereignty of grace, that he heard the doom of Sodom and Gomorrah. It was the seal of justice on the scroll of mercy. It was God warning him that he should not presume. ' By grace ye are saved, through faith, not of yourselves.' And yet, ' The soul that sinneth, it shall die.' ' Abraham,' God was saying to His child, 'it is not thy works that save thee, it is I ; yet hark to the cry of Sodom, and be warned that as a man soweth so shall he also reap.'

Have you ever been tempted to presume upon the grace of God ? I do not ask you to reply to me. I ask you to reply to your own heart. Have you ever been tempted to say, ' It does not matter much, for salvation is of grace and not of works.' Have you ever been tempted to make light of sin just because God is infinitely merciful ? Have you ever been tempted to put it off a little and have a good time just a little longer, always intending on some coming day to fall upon the arms of Jesus Christ ? By every cry that rose from Sodom I am here to warn you against that fatal error. By all that fell on beautiful Gomorrah, I warn you of the risk that you are running. Our God, the God of Abraham, the God whose grace is boundless as the sea, our God is a consuming fire. Blessed be God for His great mercy ; He willeth not that any man should perish. His grace can save you and make a saint of you although there were ten Sodoms in your heart. Only you must seek Him now, you must strip off the sin that doth beset you, you must tell Him that the deepest passion of your heart is to be a new man in Jesus Christ.

'REMEMBER Lot's wife.' We do well to re-member the occasion on which these solemn words were spoken. They were spoken when our Lord was prophesying, when He was discoursing on the hour of His return. It is often difficult in such discourses to say pre-cisely what Jesus had in view. Was it the fall of Jerusalem? Was it the end of the world? Perhaps it would be more correct to say that the fall of Jerusalem was in the foreground, but that always, in the shadowy background, there was another and a final day. Now, what Jesus here insists on is the suddenness with which that day arrives. No trumpet-note will herald its approach. Like a thief in the night it will draw near. And men will not be waiting eager and expectant any more than in the days of Noah. They will be waking and sleeping; eating and drinking; buying and selling in the market-place. Now, one might have thought that in a day like *that* one single impulse would have seized on everybody. One might have thought that every man and woman would have been heedless to all except escape. When the cry of fire rings through a crowded building, is not everything forgotten except safety? When a ship, at midnight, founders at sea, will not men and women risk everything for life? So one might have thought that in that day, when the elements are to melt with fervent heat, men and women would have been dead to everything save an uncontrollable longing to escape. But sometimes when a house has been in flames there has been some one in it who did not flee like that. And sometimes when a ship was sinking there was some one on board who was not quick to move. There was some picture there, some precious books, some little hoard of silver or gold, and even in the hour of deadly peril, have not men been known to cling to these? It was a mood like that which Jesus saw as He looked forward to His day. It was of that temper that He spake the words, 'Whosoever will save his life shall lose it.' It was then, looking back across the ages, there flashed upon His eye the doom of Sodom, and He said, 'Remember Lot's wife.'

This morning, then, we have the glad assurance that we are doing what Christ has bidden us to do. We are remembering

what He has bidden us remember. Christ
did not often use that word 'remember.'
He always used it in a serious way. It was
part of His work to sanctify the memory,
and make it a stairway to the feet of God.
'This do ye in remembrance of Me.' 'Remember the words that I have spoken unto
you.' 'Ye do not remember the loaves and
fishes.' 'Remember Lot's wife.' We have been
taught, in the writings of John Ruskin, that
it takes memory to make nature perfect.
It is only when a scene is dyed with memories
that its beauty reaches to the common heart.
So Christ taught us that memory is needed
if our religion is to be strong and beautiful.
'This do in remembrance of Me.' There is
no memory so sad but Christ can use it for
our growth in grace. There is no memory so
humiliating but Christ can use it to draw
us nearer Him. There is no memory so glad
and grateful but Christ can turn it into a
power for action. The Lord has been mindful of us, and He will bless us still.

Well then, coming to our subject, I should
like to say this to you to start with. I should
like to make it very clear to you in what
light I regard this woman's fate. I do not
regard it as a miracle. There was nothing
miraculous about it. God did not touch her

with a hand of anger and turn her into a pillar with the touch. God used the powers that were then abroad, liberated by the agency of nature ; nor was it less a judgment on her folly because it was the handiwork of nature. The soil of the spot on which she stood was of a highly bituminous and saline character. Even to-day let one but wet his lips there, and the taste of salt will be upon them. So she stood, straining her eyes to Sodom, when a sudden blast of the tempest fell upon her, and the earth was rent like a great furnace mouth with exhalations of sulphurous matter. She turned to flee, but it was now too late. She was blinded, suffocated, poisoned. It was a horrid death, not instantaneous ; it gave an awful space for wild remorse. And when those who loved her came to seek for her—for her husband and her children loved her still—like a white winding sheet of the Almighty the salt was encrusted on her body. We have read, in the story of the Alps, of bodies that have been recovered from the snow. Frozen stiff, rigid as a pillar, the ice had wrapped them round as in a garment. So after many days she would be found, but none would see the terror in her eyes, for God, who is merciful, even when He judges, had wrapped her in a mantle white as snow.

Now, it is notable that in the Book of Genesis this is the only mention of Lot's wife. Nowhere else, in the long narrative, is there the slightest notice of her name. Had Genesis been pagan literature, that would have been natural enough. We might have explained it by the mean regard that was the lot of the women of the Gentiles. But Genesis is not a pagan book. Genesis is the literature of the Jew. And the Jew, whatever faults he had, was not guilty of despising women. Why, take the story of the life of Abraham. Half of its interest depends on Sarah. We meet her constantly in tent and pilgrimage, playing her part in Abraham's career. Yet of the wife of Lot we have no tidings ; we never hear her laughing in the tent ; we never find her by her husband's side in any critical moment of his life. Had she faced the desert with him when he went out from Haran ? We should have given much to have known that. Was she the bride of his youth beyond the river, in the happy and quiet days of long ago ? Of all that we know absolutely nothing. Here is the record, and the rest is silence. And that very silence, as it seems to me, permits two opposite readings of her character.

For the first reading we must remember this.

We must remember the character of Lot. We must remember that in Lot's character there was a strange and unexplained decline. Look at him in the morning of his days. He had gone out with Abraham wholeheartedly. No one had forced him to that desert journey. He had faced it willingly and in heroic temper. There were better elements within the man, and Abraham knew them, and he loved his nephew. He would never have suffered him to follow unless he had had confidence in Lot. That is the opening of Lot's career. And then the close of it is Sodom. And in between, what is it that you find? It is rather a gradual and slow decline, a constant sinking on to lower levels, a losing of the vision and the gleam. Clearly some influence was at work on Lot that dimmed the gladness of the morning for him. It could not be Abraham with his great heart. Just as little could it be loyal Sarah. Is it not possible that it was some one dearer, with whom he had plighted troth beyond the river? Is it not possible it was his wife? She was a worldly woman at the last, and worldliness is not begotten in an hour. If she was worldly when she fled from Sodom, the seeds of it were in her when she married him. And on his pliable and easy nature, so quick to feel the tendencies of influence, a worldly woman at his side for years was all that was needed for his ruin. There are women who boast, and boast sincerely, that they always leave their husbands to their liberty. They never hamper them in any choice. They never interfere with their decisions. And yet these women, if they are coarse of heart and vulgar and just a little covetous, are influencing their husbands every day. It is likely it was so with Lot's wife. She was the secret cause of his decay. Lot never touched the mire, as David did, but he coarsened and degenerated steadily. And it is possible that in his home, as in a thousand homes from then till now, the secret lay in an unhappy marriage.

But in common justice it is right to say that we can read her character another way. It is always possible to hold that she was more sinned against than sinning. We may say, if we like, that her absence from the story shows that she was a quiet and gentle woman. She loved the shadow and the peace of home and the ceaseless prattle of the children. If so, then her husband's choice, when he chose Sodom and made his dwelling there, was the likeliest thing in the world to be her ruin. Such women, without high intelligence, are often strangely quick in intuition. They have an instinct for what is right, far surer than the logic of their husbands. And Lot was just the man to laugh at that and ridicule her scruples and her piety, and tell her, with his eye on Sodom, that a woman could know nothing of these things. Now the pity is not that a man does that, but that a woman believes him when he does it. Is it likely, she thinks, that her instinct should be right and the experience of her husband wrong? And so she comes to disbelieve herself, and to distrust the calling of her heart, and to lose that very touch of God which is the glory and guidance of her sex. Once a woman has played the traitor so, her character rapidly degenerates. Once she is laughed out of her finer feelings, she will grip Sodom closer than her husband. And I say again that Lot was just the man, with his coarse nature and his carnal eye, to mock at all that was finest in his wife. If he did it he had to pay for it, as husbands generally have to pay for it. Once let the world seize a woman's heart, and may the Lord have mercy on her husband. She married her daughters to the men of Sodom, and what the men of Sodom were you know. I can scarcely credit it that Lot would ever have suggested such alliances. Never make light, my brother, I beg of you, of the strange sensitiveness which is a woman's genius. The reasons of a woman's heart are often better than those of a man's brain. Those instincts, which they can scarcely utter, those exquisite and subtle intuitions, these are as certainly the voice of God as anything that is written in the Decalogue.

Now we come to the closing scene, and there are three features in it sadly notable. Let us follow the command of Christ, and preface each with the word ' Remember ! '

First, then, remember how nearly she was saved. Had Lot's wife perished in the city, that would have been pitiful enough. Had she fallen where the crowd lay dead, that in itself would have been tragedy. But is it not sadder that she perished here, when she was out of the city on the hills, and when life, and life with every one she loved, was, as it were, within her grasp? Everything that could be done to save her had, in the kindliness of God, been done. She had been shaken from her bed of sleep. She had been grasped by the strong hand of angels. She had been hurried through the city gate, and up the little pathway to the mountains. And that is what deepens the sadness of it all, that it was just there she was destroyed. When a ship is lost far out at sea there is always something tragic in the loss. But still more poignant is the sense of sorrow when she is wrecked on the cliffs of the homeland. When a sufferer succumbs to his disease, heavy is the sorrow of bereavement; but perhaps it is heavier when he is taken home in the day when he was almost well again. There are few things more pitiful than that. There is no spiritual tragedy more common. That was moving in the mind of Christ when He said, ' Remember Lot's wife.' You may be near the kingdom and yet not in the kingdom. You may be almost but not yet quite persuaded. 'O! the little more, and how much it is! and the little less, and what worlds away!'

Secondly, remember how loath she was to leave. Brethren, if the turning round to gaze had been an impulsive and momentary act, we might have thought, and thought perhaps with justice, that Lot's wife had met with a harsh fate. But if you will only read the passage carefully, you will never take that view of it again. The woman had been loath to leave, and she was hankering for Sodom still. Why had she not spurred her husband on, when she learned what was going to happen? Why did she need to be so taken in hand and forced away by the two angels? The fact is, that she was loath to go. She was at home in Sodom, and she loved it. She only half believed what she was told, and she could scarce tear herself from her beloved city. She loved her beautiful home and all its luxuries. She loved the excitement of the crowded street. She loved the pride of life, and the sweet music, and the fashions, and the constant gaiety. And if I am speaking to any one to-day whose life would be a desert but for such things, I want you to think that Christ is saying to you, ' Remember Lot's wife.'

Then, thirdly, remember how her fate was sealed by her desire. It wasn't what she *did* that ruined her ; it was rather what her heart was set upon. One look saved Simon Peter from impenitency, on that night when he denied his Lord. One look brought this woman to the grave when she was on the verge of liberty. And this it is that made these looks so mighty, for blessing there, and here for misery, that in both cases the heart was in the look. Brethren, in every life the deepest question is not the question of actual accomplishment. I shall go further even than that, and say it is not the question of actual transgression. The deepest question in every life is this, what kind of thing is the heart set upon ? What is the trend ? What is the direction ? What is the secret and dearest wish ? You may be a far worse man in secret hankering than another man in open sin. For he may hate his sin and hate himself, and pray to God for strength to conquer it. But you who have a name to live may have a secret and a sweet delight in it. And I tell you that it is that delight that in the long-run determines all. Blessed are they who hunger after righteousness. Cursed are they who hunger after Sodom. It is the hunger and the thirst that tell, though into Sodom you may never enter. And if I am speaking to any here to-day who in secret are living so, I would only say to you what Jesus says, 'Remember Lot's wife.'

1. It has been said by a great German theologian that our highest blessings bring our greatest trials, and it was evidently so with Abraham. Not only did this dark moment come to him after many years of great prosperity, not only, like a bolt out of the blue, did it reach him when life was at its happiest, but it reached him through the object of his love, through one who was infinitely dear to him, through the child for whom so long he had been looking, and in whom the promises were crowned. It was in the garden, amid the olive trees, that our Lord had sweetest converse with His Father. It was in that same garden, and under the same trees, that His soul was sorrowful even unto death. So Abraham, in the very sphere where he was happiest, and where life at length was as a paradise, met with his bitterest and darkest trial. Yes, as the German scholar says, our highest blessings bring our greatest trials. Just there where we have known the greatest happiness, full often do we know the greatest

sorrow. That tie, which made our life so bright and wakened us to gladness every morning, may, in the strange providence of God, become the source of our most bitter grief.

2. Observe, too, that the very greatness of the trial is a witness to the character of Abraham. There must have been something magnificent about the man whom God could test in such a way as this. When our Lord was tempted by the devil, you remember the kind of temptation that was chosen. 'All these kingdoms will I give thee, if thou wilt fall down and worship me.' And men have always felt, and rightly felt, that in the very splendour of that offer there is a testimony, however unintentional, to the splendour of the character of Christ. Now Abraham was not tempted of the devil. Abraham was tested of his God. Abraham had prayed, 'Search me, and know my heart,' and the Father was now answering that prayer. And what I say is that that severity, that unparalleled intensity of trial, is a witness of what God thought of Abraham. God is always merciful. He is the Lord God, merciful and gracious. He will not tempt a man beyond his strength. He will not break the bruised reed. And if the patriarch was tempted here as child of God has never since been

tested, it just reveals the estimate of heaven. It was a trial almost more than human. It was a trial that only God could fathom. Abraham was summoned to that very sacrifice that God made for the saving of mankind. 'For God so loved the world, that He gave His only-begotten Son, that whosoever believeth in Him should not perish, but have ever-lasting life.'

3. Let me say in passing that to appreciate this scene we must discard the standards of to-day. If we judge Abraham by our present light, his conduct is inexplicable. No Christian could contemplate such action without setting his conscience at defiance. If such a mandate were to come to us, we should reject it as a temptation of the evil one. It would be abhorrent to our better nature ; it would contradict all that was highest in us ; and you may be certain, when anything does that, that it cannot be for you the voice of God. God may summon us to trample on our feelings, but never to trample on our conscience. No outward voice can be the voice of God if it ignores the still small voice within. And taught as we are by the Gospel message, en-lightened by the spirit of Christ Jesus, it would be impossible to contemplate such action, save in defiance of the voice of conscience. Now, you

must remember that in the time of Abraham conscience had not been so educated. However deep the conflict of his feelings, there would be no conflict in his moral nature. On the contrary, all that was best in Abraham would sympathise with the demand of God, however terrible that demand might be. He had been born and bred among a people who were not ignorant of human sacrifices. He was surrounded by the Canaanites, who are known to have practised these dark rites. And while to you and me, with all our light, such sacrifices are utterly abhorrent, Abraham would view them in another way. There would come a day, as he sat by his tent door, when he would lift up his eyes and look. And afar off, beyond the hills, he would see the smoke of sacrifices rising. And he would say to himself, Think of these heathen men, worshipping a god who cannot help them, and yet so terribly in earnest over it that they have laid their sons upon the altar. And just then he would hear the voice of Isaac, singing some boyish song beside the river. And he loved the lad, the child of his old age—loved him with all his heart and soul. And the thought would flash upon him, Would I do for God what the heathen yonder are doing for their idols? Am I willing to give to God what most I love? To a great heart like his the thought was torture, and yet the torture was its fascination. He brooded on it. He became ashamed. He was letting the heathen beat him in devotion. And so the night fell, and he went to rest, and it was in the silent hours of that night that he heard a voice from heaven saying to him, Thou also must sacrifice thy son. What I want you to note is that Abraham's difficulty was not in any sense a moral difficulty. God did not contradict the best in him. God did not pour contempt upon his conscience. God seconded the verdict of his conscience ; took him at his highest and his best, and led him out of that into a larger truth that showed him how ignorant he had been.

4. On the intensity of the trial I need hardly dwell. Every father can appreciate that. Just put your son's name in in place of Isaac, and you will understand what it all meant. Note that the Scripture does not dwell on that. There is a noble reserve about the Bible. There is something almost Scottish about the narrative with its fine veiling of the deepest feelings. There is just one word about thine only son—and it is God who utters it, not Abraham—and then the veil descends, and all is quiet, and the misery and the agony are hidden. The grief of the Bible is always

quiet grief, and the grief of the Christian ought
to be so also. Christ went apart when he
would agonise, He went apart even from John
and Peter. And Abraham, with a heart all
torn and bleeding, moves like a quiet strong
man upon his journey, and he does it because
nearer than all sorrow there is the ordering and
the love of God. On the natural feelings of his
father's heart, then, the Scripture does not
choose to linger. Nor is there any need that
we should linger on what the Bible reverently
hides. But there are one or two other features
of his trial which help us to realise its bitterness,
and we must not be blind to these.

5. For instance, we must not forget that
Abraham was utterly alone. There was no
one to whom he could speak a word about this
boundless sorrow of his heart. Every one who
has had a sorrow knows what a comfort there
may be in a word of sympathy. There is
nothing that makes us feel more helpless than
a great blow falling on a friend. And yet a
grasp of the hand, a kindly visit, a word so
halting that we are ashamed of it, it is wonderful what comfort these may bring. I beg of
you, as Christian people, never to ignore these
little offices. I beg of you never to think you
can do nothing when these small sympathies
are in your power. When the flesh is sensitive

the slightest touch is felt, and when the heart is
sensitive the slightest touch is felt, and if the
touch be brotherly and gentle, you take my
word for it that it is not forgotten. Now do
you not think it deepened Abraham's burden
that there was no one who could sympathise?
Sarah knew nothing of it when he stole away.
Sarah had no idea where he was going. And
Isaac, singing and talking by his side, eager and
happy as a boy would be—what a gulf between
the father and the son. The hardest trials any
one can have are just the trials that must be
borne alone. The hardest trials are always a
little harder when those who are dearest do
not understand. And that was an element in
Abraham's trial when he went on his two days'
journey to Moriah, as it was in the journey of
Jesus to the Cross. 'Who is this that cometh
from Edom?' was what the prophet cried of
Jesus Christ. And the answer came, as from
a mist of blood, 'I have trodden the winepress
alone.' Can you wonder that Jesus, as He
thought of Abraham travelling alone to Mount
Moriah, said, 'Your father Abraham rejoiced to
see my day: and he saw it, and was glad.'

6. And then, too, to understand this testing,
you must remember that Isaac was the child of
promise. He was not only the child whom
Abraham loved. He was the child on whom

the future hung. It was through him the seed
was to be born. It was through him the world
was to be blessed. It was upon his life, and that
alone, that every promise made to Abraham
hinged. And now that son, whose life was
indispensable if the will of God was to be perfected, that son was to be slain in sacrifice. It
would have been a lighter thing to bear had
God only been contradicting Abraham. You
see that what made it intensely hard to bear
was that God seemed to be contradicting God.
And nothing better shows the faith of Abraham
than that in such an hour of divine antagonisms
he had the strength to say, My present duty is
to obey the present call of God. Brethren, the
bitterest struggles in this life are not always the
struggles between right and wrong. Sometimes the bitterest struggles of the soul are the
conflicts between right and right. When duty
clashes with interest that is a conflict, but at
least we know the thing we ought to do. It is
when duty begins to clash with duty that life
seems to be torn down to the deeps. In such
an hour remember Abraham. In such an
hour send out your thought to him. God
seemed to be contradicting God for him, yet he
had a present command and he obeyed it. And
so obeying he was led to peace, and found that
the contradiction was but seeming, saw that

there was a unity with God in which antagonisms are resolved.

7. What, then, were the results of this great
hour ? On that I should like to touch in the
last place. And to begin with, I want you to
realise what such an hour must have meant for
Isaac. Abraham is such a commanding figure
that we are to think of him, and him alone. It
is to him our sympathies go out ; it is him we
picture in that hour of testing. But what of
Isaac, and how did he behave when all in a
moment he was faced by death ? That is
an element which you must not omit. Isaac
was no longer a mere child. He had reached
now into the strength of boyhood. He was
strong enough to bear the faggots on his
shoulder as he and Abraham went up the hill.
He was old enough to know what death meant,
and in the hour when he was faced by death he
was strong enough to have fought with an old
man had his heart rebelled at being slain.
The point to note is that he did not struggle.
Quietly and willingly he gave himself. There
is not a trace of any passionate outcry, of any
wild rebellion or defiance. Trained in perfect
obedience to his father, bowing his heart before
the will of God, Isaac presented his body a
living sacrifice, holy, acceptable to God. You
could never imagine Ishmael doing that.

Ishmael would have fought like a wild beast. Ishmael would have struggled for his life, and wrestled madly for his liberty. But Isaac, who was the child of promise, yielded himself to God in full surrender, and we may say that it was in that hour that he became the spiritual heir of Abraham. It was then he learned that he that saveth his life shall lose it, and he that loseth his life for God's sake shall find it. It was then he learned that except a corn of wheat fall into the ground and die, it abideth alone. Can you not picture him rising from that altar, and taking his life as from the hand of God, and feeling as he had never felt before that God was the resurrection and the life? It was thus that a way was made for Jesus Christ. It was thus that the world was prepared for Him. Ishmael, for all his strength and all his beauty, could never possibly have been the child of promise. It was Isaac who was the child of promise. It was one who had the faith to yield himself. It was one who touched the feet of Jesus Christ by his full surrender to the will of God.

8. And then turning to Abraham, what of him? What was it that he learned in that great hour? The mightiest lesson that Abraham learned was just the deepening of his thought of sacrifice. He had gone up Moriah in the full persuasion that God demanded the slaying of

his son. He went up with the profound conviction that the death of his child was honour-
ing to God. And he came down again convinced of this, that not by the shedding of blood
is God delighted, but by the yielding of the
human will in lowly and unquestioning obedience. It was not the surrender of Isaac that
God wanted. It was the surrender of the heart
of Abraham. God did not want to rob him of
his dearest. God gave him his dearest back
again. What God demanded was a consecra-
tion so full, so universal, so complete, that
Abraham would be his and his alone. It was
that which was taught him on Moriah, when
the ram was caught in the thicket by the horns.
He saw, as he had never seen before, the sacrifice that God delighteth in. He saw it was the
sacrifice of self, the laying in the dust life's glory
dead, the inward and not the outward yielding
of all that is dearest to the heart.

9. And, brethren, the glory of that hour is
seen most wonderfully just in this, that it
became and always has remained the parable
of the sacrifice of God. We cannot think
of Abraham and Isaac but we think of the
heavenly Father and His Son. We cannot turn
our eyes to Mount Moriah but we are reminded
of another sacrifice. 'For God so loved the
world, that He gave Jesus Christ, that whoso-

ever believeth in Him should not perish.' It is of that we think, and think immediately, whenever we read of the sacrifice of Isaac. Little did Abraham know that day of the coming of Jesus Christ in human form. Little he knew of the great sacrifice when the only-begotten was so freely given. Yet acting in the obedience of faith and true to all the light that God had given him, he rose into real fellowship with that. God grant that all of us may be like Abraham, whatever we are called upon to do. When it is difficult and rends the heart, may we still have faith and courage to fulfil it. It is thus alone that we are lifted heavenward, and walk in heavenly places with Christ Jesus, and come to a living and abiding fellowship with the God and Father of our Lord Jesus Christ.

1. I SHOULD like on succeeding Sundays, till
Communion, to give you brief lectures at our
forenoon service on the Life and Work of
Nehemiah.   I wish to do so because I am afraid
that in these restless and unsettled days there
are many who have no idea of the riches of the
Old Testament.   Nehemiah is one of the finest
characters in the whole history of Judaism, a
man of extraordinary courage and at the same
time of deepest piety, one with a genius for
organising such as has been given to few, and
rich in personal attraction.   When we think of
the great patriots of history, such as William
Tell or our own Wallace, among them in
common justice we must set the name of
Nehemiah.   For truer patriot never breathed,
and this brief biography, the Book of Nehemiah,
is but patriotism in action.   In these days of
a spurious internationalism which denies to
patriotism any moral value, it is good to
company with Nehemiah.

He lived in Persia, in Susa, a rose-red city
half as old as time.   There, one day, through

a visit from his brother, he learned of the wretched condition of Jerusalem. And just as Ezra had given his life to the rebuilding of the Temple, so Nehemiah resolved to give his life to the rebuilding of the city walls. It was a task incredibly hard, as we shall see as we proceed. It called for prayer, courage, prudence, ingenuity. It demanded an unflagging spirit. And how Nehemiah held to it and wrestled with it till at last the wall was finished, is one of the finest things in Holy Scripture. In an age of little men, Nehemiah was a great man. In a period of slackened morals, Nehemiah was a man of principle. In a time when people were depressed, as so many people are depressed to-day, Nehemiah, in fellowship with God, was sustained by a hope that was unconquerable.

2. All this is the more remarkable when we remember where he was born and bred. A Jew, probably of the house of Judah, Persia was his birthplace and his home. When the Jews returned after the exile, many preferred to stay in Babylonia. They were at home there; there they had their businesses; they had prospered as Jews so often do. And in one of these families that stayed behind when the finer sort returned to Judah, Nehemiah was a child. He spent his most impressionable years in the bosom of a pagan land. Morals were loose there, and

ideals were low ; the severities of the Mosaic
law were mocked at. And yet this young
fellow, in the very heart of it, and with pagan
folk on every hand, never forgot the religion of
his fathers. The real test of a man's religion
often comes in an alien environment. The real
test is in the season when the scaffolding and
support of home are gone. Unsustained by a
surrounding atmosphere of which religion is a
vital element, how often, in distant lands, does
character go to wreck and ruin. It is a great
thing to have a godly father, perhaps a greater
to have a godly mother. But nobody is equal
to the strain of life if God, for him, be but his
father's God. Religion is a personal trans-
action, and a man's faith must be his very own,
though in the winning of it many things be lost
that were dear to father and to mother. Sooner
or later, says our Lord, we all lose what we only
seem to have. Many a person seems to have
religion because he has always been breathing a religious air. And then comes Persia
and Susa, and the dead-weight of a licentious
paganism, and religion vanishes as does a
dream. Now, of the spiritual history of Nehemiah we learn nothing in this little book.
Nehemiah in his reticence almost might have
been a Scotsman. But the point is that in a
pagan land, enervating, dissolute, luxurious,

his heart turned towards Jerusalem as steadily as the needle to the pole. He lived with the God of Abraham. He prayed to the God of Jacob. The welfare of the Holy City was dearer to him than life itself. All which is written in the Bible to encourage any who are prone to think, It is impossible for *me* to be a Christian.

3. Notable too is this, that Nehemiah was the royal cup-bearer. That implies he had a noble presence, for no other kind of man would have been tolerated. An Eastern cup-bearer, to a monarch, was an important and confidential servant. Not only did he serve the king with wine ; he had to taste it before the monarch touched it. These Eastern potentates, poor in the lap of wealth, generally dined alone and lived in continual fear of being poisoned. Thus the cup-bearer was a trusted officer. The king's life was in his hands. Very often between king and cup-bearer there were ties of very genuine friendship. And I want you to notice how that daily work, humble yet faithfully performed, led Nehemiah to the service of his life. Without the favour of King Artaxerxes Nehemiah could have accomplished nothing. Jerusalem would have remained in ruins, and the walls would never have been built. And the beautiful thing is that this great heart was led

to the service that has made his name immortal,
by his faithful and diligent discharge of the
lowly duties of a cup-bearer. He might have
treated his office cavalierly. With his high gifts,
it was beneath him. What! spend his days
serving a glass of wine, when he had a will of
iron and a heart of genius! My dear hearers, if
he'd been above his job he would never have
won the favour of the king, he'd never have
built the ramparts of Jerusalem. So many
people dream of higher service, and so dreaming, despise their present service. Ask any
employer of labour if that be not a common
cause of failure. And just here come in the
words of Jesus about being faithful in the least.
The one avenue to higher service is to be faithful in the lesser service. Perfect fidelity in little
things is God's appointed way to bigger things.
Nehemiah approved himself as cup-bearer, won
the esteem and regard of Artaxerxes, and was
so led to the service of his life.

4. Reading the story, we discover how intense was the grief of Nehemiah. The ruina-
tion of Zion broke his heart. There are many
griefs a man can hide. He can bury them in
the secret of his bosom. But there are griefs so
staggering and overwhelming that they set their
signature upon the face. And Nehemiah was
so overwhelmed by the tidings which his

brother brought him that he could not hide it
even from the king. The king noted it at once.
He spoke about it. He recognised it as sorrow
of the heart. Some mistresses never see when
their maids are looking ill, but Artaxerxes de-
tected it at once. And then followed the unexpected statement that when Nehemiah saw
his grief was known, he was sore afraid.
Afraid! Of what was he afraid? Is sympathy
a thing to be afraid of? Are men in the way
of trembling when some one speaks to them
compassionately? It is a curious insight into
Eastern courts, not without significance, that
Nehemiah at once suspected danger when the
king made remark upon his grief. Don't you
see, in the presence of the king one was always
expected to be happy. Grief was banished by
the royal favour. There was nothing but sunshine in the monarch's presence. And though
that, with Oriental tyrants, was nothing but a
fiction of the court, our Lord taught us that it
was not a fiction with the loving sovereignty
of heaven. To live as in the eye of God, to
view things under the aspect of eternity, to
realise that One who loves us infinitely is constantly watching ; this, the secret of the life of
Jesus, is a secret that brings gladness when the
burden is heavy and the cross is sore. 'In Thy
presence is fulness of joy.' That was why

Nehemiah was afraid. To be gloomy in the presence of the king was at once an insult and a treachery. And then the Psalmist, who knew these Eastern sovereigns, contrasted them with the sovereign in heaven, and wrote out of a grateful heart, ' In Thy presence is fulness of joy.' We do not make enough of the gladness of Christianity. Christianity conquered through its gladness. ' Rejoice in the Lord : and again I say, Rejoice.' We should be none the worse of being afraid sometimes, just as Nehemiah was afraid, when we are gloomy, heavy-eyed, and heavy-hearted in the presence of the King.

5. Again, I ask you to note that illuminating touch that we have in the fourth verse : ' So I prayed unto the God of heaven.' Now please use your imagination and picture to yourselves the scene. It was the great hour of Nehemiah's life. All his future depended upon that hour. He is about to proffer a very bold petition. He wants an appointment as Governor of Judah. And the first thing that Nehemiah does is not to proffer his petition : it is to pray unto the God of heaven. He had only an instant for that prayer. Silence would have been mis-interpreted. Had he closed his eyes and lingered in devotion, the king immediately would have suspected treason. One inward cry, one arrow-flight to heaven, that was

the compass of his opportunity, and Nehemiah caught at it and gripped it. I wonder what he prayed for. I wonder what he packed into that instant. I hope some day to be told in heaven the infinite riches of that little room. But the difference that moment made Nehemiah never could forget, and that is why it is here in his biography. That prayer put words into his mouth. It gave him the right tone in which to utter them. The answer to that prayer was given instantly in the gracious acquiescence of the king. A single swift arrow-flight to heaven for the right word, and the right tone, and the right temper—that made all the difference in the world. How different our lives would be if we all practised ejaculatory prayer. Had we touched heaven for a single instant, what remorse we should have saved ourselves. How many letters would never have been posted, how many words would never have been spoken, which, spoken, can never be recalled. It was a counsel we used to get in childhood to count ten before we spoke. Had Nehemiah waited till he had counted ten he would have had a dagger in his breast. He did better; he waited upon God for a single swift unnoticeable instant, and in that instant built the walls of Zion. To do that every day is one of the great secrets of the saints. No habit is more blessed than that of ejaculatory prayer. An arrow-flight to heaven before you say that word or pay that visit binds your day about the feet of God. It was there that Nehemiah lived. It was there he saved his soul alive. No man ever felt more deeply that the hand of God was on him all the time.

And so we leave him for a week, to join him again next Sunday morning building the ruined ramparts of Jerusalem.

1. No account has been given us of the journey of Nehemiah to Jerusalem. There is a great deal of travelling in the Bible, but the Bible is not a book of travel. The only journeys enlarged upon in Scripture are the missionary journeys of St. Paul. But these were not journeys towards a goal : in Paul's case the journey *was* the goal. The Bible is not a book of travel ; and when Abraham, Jacob, Nehemiah travel, we are carried from start to finish in a sentence. From Susa to Jerusalem would take the traveller two months at the shortest. His road would lie across a desert, and then through the beauty of Damascus. But, to a pious Jew like Nehemiah, even Damascus would be forgotten when his eyes rested on Jerusalem. American travellers tell us of the first impression made on them by England. They have heard since childhood of the famous places, they have imagined the historic scenes. But to see, for the first time, what they have dreamed about a thousand times stirs them in a way that no foreigner can understand. So would it be with Nehemiah when Jerusalem first broke upon his

gaze. For him it was no alien city. A thousand times, like Daniel, when he had gone apart to pray in Susa, he had opened his windows towards Jerusalem. There David had had his throne. There Solomon had reigned in splendour. There, by the will of God, the Temple rose. There were his fathers' sepulchres. How profound would the impression be on the heart of this true patriot when for the first time he looked and saw Jerusalem. When, one summer morning, Jesus saw it, the tears coursed down His cheeks. He saw, in His mind's eye, its coming ruin. But Nehemiah saw its actual ruin, that first morning when he gazed upon it, and I do not think his tears were far away. These ruins he had to restore. That was the task which brought him there. The one burning ambition of his heart was to rebuild Jerusalem. And how he did it, how wisely and how bravely, I now proceed to show you.

2. The first thing which Nehemiah did is very characteristic of the man. It was to make himself thoroughly acquainted with the range of the desolation. He would not take anything on hearsay, even though the informant was his brother. He would see things with his own eyes ; he must investigate matters for himself. And so one night, when everything was dark, unattended save by a faithful few, he made the

circuit of the walls.   I sometimes wonder that
no painter has given us a picture of that
incident.   Nehemiah, in the night, amid the
ruins.   The desolation of it all was terrible.
It was a scene of chaos.   Everywhere, ruined
masonry and debris, and burned and blackened
gates.   And it is characteristic of the man that
with his own eyes he must see that desolation
before he took in hand to set things right.   If
people took the trouble to do that we should
have less tinkering with social reforms.   There
would be no more tinkering with the drink
traffic if statesmen saw the ravages of drink.
The first step in social reform is in the darkness
to go round the ruins and let the horror of it
seize upon the spirit.   No man will ever know
how boundless is our debt to Christianity till
he acquaints himself with the moral desolation
of the pagan world to which it came.   It was
because God saw the ruin sin has caused, as no
human eye can ever see it, that He did not put
us off with shallow remedies, but gave us His
own Son to be Redeemer.   It has been said that
the miracle of Shakespeare is his fidelity to fact.
He explores the ruins of humanity, as Nehemiah
the ruins of Jerusalem.   And yet, like Nehemiah,
he is never hopeless, never indulges the cowardice
of pessimism, sees a budding morrow in midnight.   Had Nehemiah rushed into the work

on the report and information of his brother, my
humble impression is that the whole business
would have come to nothing. But he saddled his
mule, and rode into the night and saw the desolation for himself, and like Livingstone among the
slavers, what he saw kept him glowing to the end.

3. I like to note again that for this restoration
no *new* material was needed. In the debris of
the ruined masonry lay all the material required. True, for the gates new wood was
needed, for the gates had been consumed with
fire. And Nehemiah had permission, you
remember, to get all the timber he wanted
from the forester. But for the walls there was
no need of new material, all that was needed
was lying in the ruins ; and it seems to me that
is always so when the walls of Zion are rebuilt.
Luther rebuilt the walls of Zion, and will you
tell me how he accomplished that ? Was it
by proclaiming what was new ? by using what
was never used before ? Martin Luther did
precisely what Nehemiah did : he took the old
stones among the ruins, and with them he reformed the Church. Was justification by faith
a new conception ? It was old as the apostle
Paul. It had been the glory of the earliest
Church and the earliest hope of the despairing
sinner. And what Luther did was to take that
saving doctrine out of the hideous ruins at his

feet, and with it rebuild the walls of Zion. For a revived and restored Church we want nothing that is new. What we want is a new spirit, never a new material. In the old doctrines, in the ancient truths, in the old, old story of the grace of God, we have all the material that is needed for the restoration of Jerusalem. Whenever a revival comes we find ourselves side by side with Nehemiah. We cease quarrying for new material. All we need is in the ruined debris, in things we learned when we were children, in truths that the apostles knew, in hopes and musics that are as old as Calvary. I am, I trust, no obscurantist. I have no objection to being called a modernist. But I confess I haven't the least hope for Zion unless she builds her walls of the old stones.

4. I ask you to notice further that in the restoration all kinds of people were employed. Every citizen must lend a hand, as well as the inhabitants of neighbouring villages. In our day no one would be allowed to build unless he belonged to a trade union. In that day there were no trade unions, although there were the rudiments of guilds. Nehemiah was at liberty to insist on the services of everybody, and that is exactly what he did. Had he left the matter to professional builders the work would never have been finished. Bricklayers and masons

took their share, but skilled tradesmen had to be supplemented. Nehemiah set every one to work, called upon the services of everybody, and so doing rebuilt the walls of Zion. There, labouring, were proud aristocrats and the humble peasants from the villages. There were the priests toiling at the building, and not far away from them were the Levites. There were the singers and the porters, and the apothecaries and the goldsmiths, and the merchants, and the loafers from the market-place. Very probably the nobles said, 'This kind of thing is beneath us.' And the goldsmiths, with their delicate fingers, would protest that they could not trundle stones. But Nehemiah, like all great organisers, had his own way of dealing with excuses, and of inspiring folk to lend a hand. Now, if I know anything of Scripture, that isn't here just as a bit of history. You must never forget that the history of Scripture is meant of God to be prophetical. It is here because always where Jerusalem is to be built the services of every one are needed. Take the condition of the Church to-day. Men call it decadent and powerless. And then, they blame the ministers, or as frequently the office-bearers. But to us Protestants the Church is not the clergy, it is the whole body of confessing people, and the censure directed to the pulpit is just as applicable to the pew. Nehemiah did not ask the priests to do the whole business of rebuilding. He called on every citizen of Zion from the humblest up to the aristocrat. And Zion never will regain her ramparts of spiritual authority and power till that old procedure is repeated. Not till everybody lends a hand, not till every pew is serving, not till every communicant is saying 'Here am I, use me,' can we ever hope to see the Church coming up out of the wilderness, fair as the sun, clear as the moon, terrible as an army with banners.

5. It is deeply interesting to notice also where the citizens were put to work. Each was set to labour on the bit of wall opposite his home. We are told, for instance, that the priests repaired each over against his house, and the wisdom of that course is manifest. It prevented the confusion of hurrying and meeting crowds. It saved a deal of time, when the trumpet sounded to begin. It deepened the interest of every worker in the bit of work that he was doing : in toiling for Jerusalem he was toiling for home and wife and children. That, you remember, was how Jesus built. He came to found a universal kingdom. Yet He did not begin with the Greeks or the barbarians. He began with the bit over against His house—with the fishermen upon the loch, with the lowly villagers of

Galilee, with the crowds outside the cottage where He slept. I do not say that men are not called to service in far distant places. Every missionary would contradict that statement— Livingstone, Chalmers, Donald Fraser. But I do say that for the vast majority the task that God appoints is the task lying at the door. The nearest thing is God's thing. The nearest duty is God's duty. He who cannot find his service there is little likely to be useful anywhere. To repair over against one's house, at home, in one's familiar neighbourhood, is the way to the rebuilding of Jerusalem. I beg you, especially you younger people, not only to dream of service far away. If you are called to that, God bless you. There is no mistaking that summons when it comes. Meantime here is Glasgow, with its problems, with its slums, with its temptations, and the question for every patriot is this, Are you repairing over against your own house? Over against your own house there is a public-house : have you done anything to get that suppressed ? Over against your office is a slum : have you done anything to get that slum demolished ? Over against your house are cripple children and folk whose lives are un-utterably grey : have you ever brought there a gleam of sunshine? People blame me sometimes for immersing my life in Wellington. I ought to have larger interests, and do this or that, and serve on committees, and what not. I beg my critics to remember that while God requires a hundred forms of service, the man who repairs over against his house is needed for the rebuilding of Jerusalem.

6. In closing, I ask you to remember one great fact that might escape you. This great work would never have been done but for the presence in its midst of Nehemiah. Methods were excellent, organisation admirable, the business side of things was ably handled. But all the organisation in the world would never have restored Jerusalem. For that, back of organisation, was needed always an inspiring presence, and blessed be God, that inspiring presence is moving amid our ruined walls to-day. Nehemiah could not be everywhere. Our blessed Saviour can be everywhere. Nehemiah was recalled ; our blessed Saviour never is recalled. And back of all our service we need Him, encouraging, directing, and inspiring, if Zion is to be a glory once again. Without Him we can do nothing though we toil from morning sun till dark. With Him, in fellowship with Him, we can do all things.

Blessed Lord, help us to feel Thy presence, to hear Thy voice, to catch Thine inspiration, that our labour in the Lord be not in vain.

1. I SPOKE to you in my last lecture of the building of the wall, and of the various steps which Nehemiah took to reconstruct the ramparts of the city. If all this were but a tale of history, there would have been little use repeating it. The pulpit is not a Chair of History. But, as I trust you all agree with me, the history of the Bible is prophetical, and so written for our admonition. If the doom of Sodom, the exodus and exile, the fall of Jericho, the rebuilding of Jerusalem—if such events were only facts of history, they would be profoundly interesting to the student. But it seems to me one must be very stupid who, reading these narratives in Scripture, does not catch in them the word of God to *him*. Children are taught to read in large letters. Tiny little letters baffle them. And there are pictures in children's lesson-books to illustrate the text. So God, who is our Father and who knows the weakness of His bairns, gives pictures in His lesson-books and writes in the capitals of history.

2. Now the work which Nehemiah wrought

was carried out amid various discouragements, and it is of these discouragements that I want to speak a little while this morning. No good work is ever wrought save in the face of multiplied discouragements. The work of our blessed Lord was carried through in the teeth of a hundred obstacles and barriers. And it is well to remember, whenever we set our hand to anything for the welfare of our fellows, that the servant is not greater than his Lord. In the training of children, in striving for the franchise, in all endeavour for a better country, in seeking to elevate the fallen, in wrestling for the disarmament of nations—always there are discouragements, just as there were for Christ, for the servant is not greater than his Lord. The singular thing is how these discouragements answer to those of Nehemiah. The weapons of man alter with the centuries, but the weapons of the devil are unchanged. The devil is not the least original, and he still uses in the twentieth century the shafts which he hurled at Nehemiah. What these were, and how he threw them I now propose to show you.

3. First, then, I ask you to observe that Nehemiah had trouble with his workmen. That has a curiously familiar sound to employers of labour who are here this morning. Men speak sometimes as if industrial troubles

were peculiar to our own industrial era. It is
in such matters that a little knowledge of history
is often such an excellent corrective. When there
was no machinery and no industrialism, and
no socialism, save that of God, Nehemiah
had trouble with his workmen. To-day such
trouble shows itself in strikes ; in Nehemiah's
time it was pretty much the same. His men
grew weary, they lost heart ; they ceased to
have any interest in their work. Oppressed by
the continual routine, gaining no advantage by
their industry, they came perilously near to
downing tools, a procedure we are familiar
with to-day. Nehemiah's trouble with his
workmen was not that they wanted higher
wages. As a matter of fact, they didn't get any
wages in the rebuilding of Jerusalem. His
trouble was that they grew weary, and lost both
their interest and their vision, as though their
labour in the Lord was in vain.

4. Now, in all high endeavour that discouragement is prevalent. There are men who
start enthusiastically, and then the enthusiasm
dies away. Perhaps there is no better test of
people than how they act when enthusiasm
vanishes. No sea is always at full tide ; in
every ocean is an ebb. And how one acts in
the ebb-tide of life, and when life is bounded
by miseries and shallows, is one of the surest

marks of character. It is a bad sign when any one gives up then and loses heart, and ceases from endeavour. It is a bad sign when one is only hopeful when the tide is at the full. To continue serving when the tide is out, to keep on keeping on, is the one way to the music and the stars. In the log-book of Columbus there is one entry more common than all others. It is not, ' To-day we saw the land.' It is, ' To-day we sailed on.' And to sail on, to live on, to serve on, when everything is pretty hopeless, is the only route for reaching the new world. Never forget that the higher you ascend, the more you are in the sphere of fluctuations. The mountains never change, but the breast of the loch is for ever changing. The mud is mud from morning sun till dark, but rise upward to the human heart and you have the fluctuations of its beating. Character is largely built through the mastery of fluctuations. Every man has moments on the mount, and his hours in the shadows of the glen. It is good to remember that the God who loves us is not only a God of the hills, but is God of the hills and of the valleys.

5. Then will you please note the point of time at which these workers were discouraged. We learn that it was at the middle of the work. It is in little touches such as this that I discover

the mark of inspiration ; I recognise a writer
who knows me. At the beginning of the work
there was a great enthusiasm in the workers.
And then at the end, when the mighty task was
finishing, you find a recurrence of that spirit.
The testing time, the time of difficulty, the
time when despairing was not far away, was
when the great endeavour was half-done. Just
then, midway in the business, when the glow
of the beginning was departed ; just then, when
the end was not in sight yet, and nobody had a
vision of the goal—just then came the discouragement, and the peril of the sinking heart,
and the wonder if it was all worth while. I
believe that in all the highest service the mid-
point is the point of strain. It is so with the
artist when he paints his picture. It is so with
the preacher when he writes his sermon. It is
so, as you shall find in history, in every effort
for social reform. It is so in missionary enter-
prise. Missions began in a romantic fashion.
There is the thrill and daring of the individual.
They are going to end, if we believe the Bible,
in the conquest of the world. But in between,
at the mid-point, and when committees are
smothering romance, you have the hard time
in the building of the Kingdom, as in the rebuilding of Jerusalem. Thomas à Kempis said,
'Resist beginnings.' It is most excellent advice.

For myself, I have to cry as often, ' Resist the middle point.' It is then the heart sinks and the glow is gone. It is then that doggedness is needed. It is then the worker must have faith in God.

6. And as it is, very generally, in all high and valiant endeavour, so is it, we must not forget, in the gradual unrolling of our lives. The mid-point, the middle period, the time when the building of life is half accomplished, is often a season of discouragement. One hears many sermons to young men, and there are excellent reasons for such sermons. For youth is life's determinative period, and sets the trend for all the days to come. If you capture youth you take the citadel ; if you win youth, you win the life ; if you inspire the energies of youth, you can strike out the word ' Impossible.' The strange thing is that you hear so little preaching on the perils of the middle-aged. For one sermon to the middle-aged you shall have a hundred to young men. Yet in the building up of life, as in the building of that old Jerusalem, there are perils in the middle period which, to forget, is folly. The enthusiasm of youth is gone, and with it idealism is apt to go. Men settle down, they cling to their routine, they have found their life-work, and are busy at it. And while this is good, and brings a

quiet happiness to which youth is so often a
stranger, it has dangers peculiarly its own.
Once, when talking to a farmer I was pitying
his horses at the plough. It was an upland
farm, the fields were very steep, the horses had
to struggle up the brae. But the farmer told
me that these hilly fields were not nearly so
trying to the horses as the long steady pull upon
the level. In walking, as every walker knows,
it is the long straight road that tires. There is
no surprise in it, no unexpectedness, no sudden
view, no dip into the glen. And for most
people the middle part of life is the level and
often dusty part, where the feet are very prone
to weary. We all start walking on the hills.
That is why youth is perennially needed. We
all go down into the glen, at last, and hope to
find Him on the other side. But for us, as for
the builders of Jerusalem, the half-way point,
the period in the middle, is the period when the
heart is apt to tire. Do you remember how the
Psalmist speaks of the destruction that wasteth
at noonday ? There is an arrow that flieth in
the dark ; there is a destruction that wasteth at
noonday. A poet always thinks in pictures,
and in that picture of the inspired poet you see
the perils of the middle-aged. The loss of
faith in man, which is but a step to the loss of
faith in God, the silent, steady hardening of the

heart, the decay of vision till the eyes are holden—this, with a tendency to grosser sins and an increasing emphasis on money, is the destruction that wasteth at noonday. In their own way, at their own task, this peril met the builders of Jerusalem. Half-way through the devil met them, for discouragement is always of the devil. And it seems to me that all this is in Scripture, however the higher critics may explain it, because the history of Scripture is prophetical.

7. Lastly, will you please observe how Nehemiah mastered this discouragement. He didn't do it by threatening to shoot. He did it by calling in the prophets. There were prophets there like Haggai. They were burning with the Word of God. The workmen might be hopeless ; the prophet had God's hope. And Nehemiah, genius as he was, recognised that for industrial troubles there was little hope but in the Word of God. For us, that Word is Christ. The Word has become flesh and dwelt among us. The Word that the prophets spoke in broken syllables has become flesh, and dwelt among us. And I believe that in this age of ours, out of despair is dawning a new sense, that there is little hope for our industrialism save in listening to that Word. To explore the mind of Christ, resolutely to apply it, to banish selfish-

ness and exalt service, to look on men as ends and not as means; this, increasingly to thoughtful people, is becoming the only avenue of hope to a rebuilt and regenerated world. It certainly was so to Nehemiah, and Nehemiah was a man of genius. He saw there was no issue from his troubles save through the Word of God. And you have this story in the Bible, not as an interesting bit of history, but because all Scripture, given by inspiration, is profitable for reproof and for correction.

When I began the preparation of this sermon there was a great deal more I meant to say. You will note I haven't said a word yet of the opposition and Nehemiah's exercises. One never knows, handling the Bible, where the Spirit of God is going to detain him. But one thing I do know is this, that to overfeed a congregation is as bad as to overfeed a bairn. So, with your permission, I shall leave all that till the next time I am preaching in the morning.

1. LAST morning I spoke to you of the opposition Nehemiah met with, not from his enemies, but from his fellow-workers. To-day I have to speak to you on the opposition of his enemies, and I do so for reasons of encouragement. Spiritual work is never easy, whether for the world or in the heart. To attain, as the hymn puts it, one has to wrestle 'gainst storm and wind and tide. And God, I take it, selects these ancient histories, for the Book which is our rule of life, that we may be heartened by what we see in others. I know, as well as anybody, the vast debt we owe to higher criticism. But we shall never understand the Bible if our only attitude be critical. The Bible is like our brother, and nobody ever understands his brother who is continually criticising him. Take the old Bible—or the new Bible—for the soul, it does not matter which. Take the Bible of your childhood, or the Bible reset in modern knowledge, and then sit down before it like a child, and hear what God the Lord will speak, if you want to know its inspiration. When you

do that it finds you, as no other book has ever done. When you do that, it doesn't teach you service, it teaches you you're a hell-deserving sinner. It lays you low, it lifts you up, it crowns you with the promises of God, which are yea and amen in Jesus Christ.

2. The first thing, then, we note is this, in studying the good work of Nehemiah, that always, from the first day to the last, he was surrounded by suspicious eyes. Nehemiah made no secret of the work that he was set to do. He was called of God to it ; it was a work of conscience. But all the time, not very far away, were men and women who utterly distrusted him and viewed his every action with suspicion. Everything he did they misinterpreted. They read their own hearts into his motives. Themselves disappointed, embittered and callous, they attributed their littleness to him. Every morning, hastening to his work, he was ringed round by the suspicious eyes of a multitude who never raised a finger. It is a pleasant and delightful thing to work amid sweet appreciation. When we are appreciated we do our best, and sometimes even better than our best. But to toil on, from day to day, when malevolent and suspicious eyes are watching, *that* is the persistence of the hero. Now that is just what Nehemiah did. You have only to

read the story to discover it. Suspected, un-
appreciated, he was gallant, generous, eager to
the end. And I take it that God has put the story
here, in the Book which is our rule of faith and
life, that some forlorn and shipwrecked brother
seeing, may take heart again. If I speak to
any one this morning who feels he is misunder-
stood, to any one who has to face the day without a single appreciative word—think of this
gallant heart, always surrounded by suspicious
eyes, and yet indomitably holding to it. 'Persistence,' says Emerson, 'is the characteristic of the
hero.' To keep on keeping on is the surest proof
that you are kept. Sunny hours are not the test
of character. The test of character is the bad
day, when the keepers of the house do tremble,
and the daughters of music are brought low.

3. Probably it was some such thought as that
that made our Lord love the Book of Nehemiah.
One pictures Him stealing to the church at
Nazareth and feasting His youthful soul upon
its pages. Our fathers used to preach upon the
types, and we are none the better because we
seldom do it. For certainly, in this respect at
any rate, Nehemiah was a type of Christ. I
ask you to think of the suspicious eyes that
continually surrounded Jesus. Men misinterpreted everything He did ; still worse, they
misinterpreted Himself. He was a gluttonous

man ; He was a winebibber ; He cast out
devils by Beelzebub ; they even ventured to
hint that He was mad.   Once He went into the
synagogue, where stood the man who had the
withered hand.   And the Gospel tells us that
they watched Him, to see if He would heal upon
the Sabbath.   They watched Him—they were
always watching Him, just as they always did
with Nehemiah, with malignant and suspicious
eyes.   It is a beautiful thing to be continually
watched by eyes of love, as when a mother
watches, or a father, with eyes that shine with
tenderness and pride.   But to be watched
daily, in everything one does, with eyes that
are only bent on finding fault, must be one of
the sorest disciplines of life.   It is so apt to make
the spirit bitter, so apt to bring the rasp into the
voice, so apt to chill the heart and curdle all
the milk of human kindness.   And the perfectly wonderful thing about our Lord is that,
so surrounded by suspicious eyes, He went on,
genial and kindly and infinitely loving, to the
end.   He never grew cynical nor bitter.   There
never came the rasp into His voice.   He was as
tender and as full of gladness as if every man
He met had been His friend.   I wonder, in
those dark days of His, when fierce suspicions
beat upon His brow, if He thought on Nehemiah
and was comforted.

4. But not only was Nehemiah suspect : he was assailed, also, with the shafts of ridicule. They tried to stop his work by laughing at him. No doubt there was something highly ludicrous in these grave seigniors trying to be masons. It must have been delightfully diverting to see the apothecary playing builder. Why, said the enemies, if a fox come up at night and only brush his tail against the wall, the whole thing will go tumbling in ruin. It has often been noted that the sting of ridicule is most keenly felt when we are young. ' He was one of those young fellows,' says Thackeray, ' who could not bear to be laughed at.' I have known young fellows who weren't in the least annoyed if they were considered to be just a little wicked, but I never met one who could bear to be ridiculed. Now the point is that Nehemiah was young. Only a youth could act as Persian cup-bearer. And not only youths, but very handsome youths, who liked themselves to be taken very seriously. It was a real, a very real temptation, such as we older folk can hardly understand, when Nehemiah, for the first time in his life, found that every one was laughing at him. Had he been a weakling he would have struck his colours. That is what the weakling always does. But Nehemiah, exquisitely sensitive, was not the kind of man to strike his colours.

He nailed them to the mast. He let the winds of ridicule unfurl them, and quietly he kept on keeping on. Many of us are old enough to remember the early story of the Salvation Army : how it was jeered at, how it was mocked, what floods of ridicule were poured upon it. And yet last Sunday, from an Army lassie we had as beautiful a tale of work for Christ as I have ever heard from woman's lips. General Booth was just like Nehemiah. He kept on keeping on. Assailed by a perfect storm of ridicule, he held to his conviction and his duty. All which is given us (in Scripture) to strengthen us when tempted to be cowardly, and to strike the colours of our conscience.

5. And here again I ask you to observe how Nehemiah was a type of Christ. No one can read the Gospels without seeing how Jesus was assailed with ridicule. When a man is loved his nature opens, as a berry does under the summer sun. When a man is hated that very hate may brace him, as the storm braces the fir tree of the Highlands. But when a man is ridiculed, only the grace of heaven can keep him courteous, reverent and tender, and our blessed Lord was ridiculed continually. Men ridiculed His origin. ' Can any good thing come out of Nazareth ? ' Men ridiculed His words, they laughed Him to scorn in Jairus'

house. Men ridiculed his actions. ' He casteth out devils by Beelzebub.' Men ridiculed his claim to be Messiah. Recall that hour when, bleeding and forspent, Jesus was brought out before the people. And Pilate cried, ' Behold your king ! ' Isn't that broken dreamer like a Caesar ? That, and the robe of purple, and the sceptre, and the crown of thorns, is it not the cruellest ridicule of history ? And then remember Jesus was still young, just as Nehemiah was still young. And yet more, being sinless, Jesus was exquisitely sensitive. For sin is coarsening and dulls the heart ; and, as our own poet has poignantly expressed it, ' It hardens a' within, and petrifies the feeling.' All this was known to Jesus just as it was known to Nehemiah. No little part of the cross he had to bear was the loud, cruel ridicule of men. And yet, like Nehemiah, He went on, and set His face steadfastly towards Jerusalem, and was trustful and loving to the end.

6. There is only one more thing I have to say on the opposition Nehemiah met with. It is that when everything else failed, his enemies tried to work upon his fears. They tried to make him suspect, and that failed. The man kept striving though the dogs were barking. They tried to pierce him with the shafts of ridicule, and the shafts made no impression on his armour. Then, having failed in every other way, they tried to

work upon his fears. Whispers reached him
that he was in peril. There was a plot afoot for
his assassination. Let him fly for sanctuary to
the Temple, if he didn't want to lose his life. I
know no finer words in history than those of
Nehemiah then. 'Should such a man as I flee?'
In the journal of Dr. Livingstone there is one
sentence that can never die. Ill, solitary, his
medicine chest lost, he writes, ' I am immortal
till my work is done.' And Nehemiah, like
Dr. Livingstone, when everything was threatening, felt he was immortal till his work was done.
' Should such a man as I flee ? ' ' I am doing
a great work, I cannot come down.' Had
he fled, he'd have been stabbed in treachery.
He knew he was safest on the path of duty.
And one of the lessons we have all to learn in
a life beset by spiritual enemies is that the path
of duty is the safest. Christian, in Bunyan's
Pilgrim's Progress, turned aside into Bypath
Meadow. It was easy going there and pleasant,
and you could hardly see the grass for flowers ;
but there—not on the flinty road—there, the
day he left the road, he found himself in the
grip of Giant Despair, and was made prisoner
in Doubting Castle. Nehemiah was wiser than
Christian. ' Should such a man as I flee ? '
His enemies tried to work upon his fears, but
Nehemiah kept resolutely on. All which is
written so that when days are dark and the

heart fails, and fears are round about us, we may pluck up heart again and keep the road.

7. And here again, most singularly, Nehemiah is a type of Christ. For men tried to work upon His fears, just as they did on those of Nehemiah. Did not the Pharisees come to Him and say, Get away from here, for Herod wants to kill you? And did not our Lord reply, Go, tell that fox, I am immortal till My work is done? No suspicion, no ridicule, no fears could turn the Lord from His appointed road, though the end of it was the Cross upon the hill. My dear hearer, there are many ways in which you may be tempted from the right. You may be eyed askance, you may be ridiculed, you may be warned of most disastrous consequences. But whether at home, or in the routine of business, or in preaching, or service for the kingdom, I bid you take your stand and shame the devil. Nehemiah did it, and he built the wall. Christ did it, and He rose again. Neither suspicion nor ridicule nor fear could deflect them from their purpose. And if you and I, in our own humble way, hold to the right when it is very difficult, we shall be in the glorious company of those for whom the trumpets sound upon the other side.